GLENN MURCUTT
works and projects

GLENN MURCUTT

works and projects

FRANÇOISE FROMONOT

THAMES AND HUDSON

Translated from the French by Alexandra Campbell

English translation copyright © 1995 Thames and
Hudson, London, and Whitney Library of Design,
an imprint of Watson–Guptill Publications/
New York

First published in Great Britain in 1995 by
Thames and Hudson Ltd, London

Copyright © 1995 by Electa, Milano
Elemond Editori Associati

British Library Cataloguing-in-Publication Data
A catalogue record for this book is available from
the British Library

ISBN 0-500-27852-0

Printed and bound in Italy

Contents

Preface   7

Part One
Background and Influences   11

FORMATIVE YEARS   12

MIES AND CHAREAU   17

THE AUSTRALIAN TRADITION   25

NATURE AND LANDSCAPE   31

Part Two
Principles and Themes   38

THE ARCHITECT-ARTISAN   38

ARCHITECTURAL TYPOLOGY   39

AIR, WATER AND LIGHT   44

AN ECOLOGICAL FUNCTIONALISM   48

Part Three
Selected Buildings and Projects

Biographical Notes   157

Buildings and Projects   158

Bibliography   160

Preface

Glenn Murcutt is the first Australian architect whose work has attracted such international interest. On the other side of the world, he has patiently been producing works of remarkable consistency, strikingly unusual yet curiously familiar, almost exclusively domestic in character. In 1992 he won the seventh Alvar Aalto medal, previously awarded to Aalto himself, Jørn Utzon, Alvaro Siza and Tadao Ando – those who have 'sought to marry modern architecture to the place, the territory, the landscape',[1] in Murcutt's words. The jury, which comprised prominent theorists and practitioners of Critical Regionalism,[2] specifically praised the 'convincing synthesis of regional characteristics, climate-conditioned solutions, technological rationality and unconstrained visual expression'.

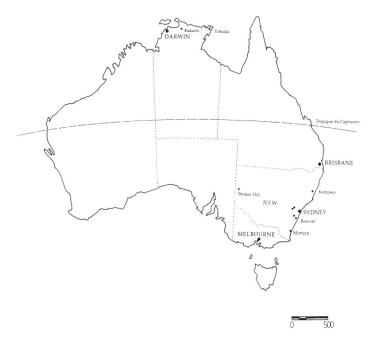

Murcutt is very courteous, quick and intense. Of strong convictions, he is eager to get his message across and almost liable to preach in lectures or interviews on subjects close to his heart. Sociable by nature but a socialite by necessity, he is gratified by his increasing reputation while considering it perhaps something of a burden. Dogged, disciplined, rigorous, he prefers to observe and understand the mechanisms of tangible phenomena to better delight in the poetry he finds there. Neither bookish nor theoretical, he is a tireless advocate of the 'science of the concrete'.

How, then, does he work? What explains his unique cast of mind, fuels his inspiration, compels him to run his practice in such an unusual manner? How can we best approach his oeuvre to reveal both its subtle evolution and pronounced 'invariants'? What is the genesis of his arresting forms – deceptively simple, unfailingly elegant, appearing as if they had landed on sites to which they will seemingly never conform?

The Architecture of Glenn Murcutt

Magney House
Bingi Point, New South Wales, 1983–85.
Preliminary sketch

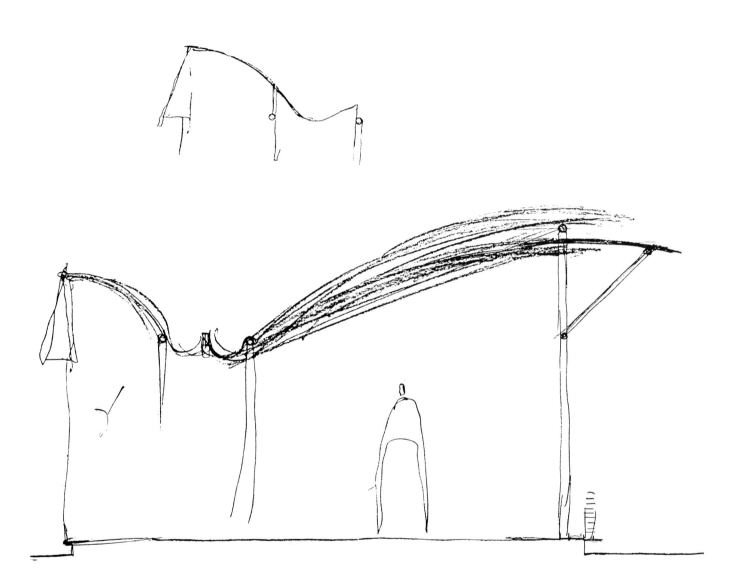

Part One

Background and Influences

A close examination of the broad framework within which Murcutt has lived and worked allows us to disentangle the confusion of influences woven into the fabric of his work. While he himself tends to single out those forces he is most directly conscious of, the place and time of his architectural education, Sydney during the 1950s and 1960s, undoubtedly exposed him to both local and foreign perspectives embedded with a number of the ideas he went on to develop in a highly personal manner.

After the Second World War, Australia entered a period of economic and urban growth that rapidly generated a renaissance in the domestic architecture for the newly created suburbs. Contacts and exchanges between Australian architects and the rest of the world decisively influenced events in a relatively isolated continent whose recent origins and colonial past still kept it closely dependent on British culture. Following the involuntary expatriation of Australian architects during the Depression years, it became a ritual for young architects to seek professional experience in Europe or the United States. They returned with first-hand information on architectural history and trends in Western architecture. Since the late 1930s, Australia had also received the input of European architects fleeing Nazism. Harry Seidler, who became the most famous, had left his native Vienna for America, where he studied under Walter Gropius and later worked with Marcel Breuer, and Oscar Niemeyer in Brazil, before settling in Sydney in 1948. An abundance of material on current American architecture was increasingly reaching Australia: *Architectural Forum*, *Architectural Record* and *Pencil Points* (later *Progressive Architecture*) disseminated the latest developments, focusing on the legendary figures of Frank Lloyd Wright and the exiled masters of the Bauhaus and their many followers. Under the editorship of John Entenza, the innovative Los Angeles magazine *Arts and Architecture* published its Case Study Houses program, discovered Rudolph Schindler and Luis Barragán, and popularized with 'design' the idea that modern aesthetics was applicable to furniture and other household objects. Magazines were

also launched in Sydney and Melbourne. *Architecture and Arts*, for instance, deliberately mirrored the prestigious Californian journal, even adopting a similar layout.[3] In all these publications emerged the leitmotif of rapidly expanding suburban cultures on both sides of the Pacific: the potential for modern architecture's contribution to the private house and the art of living.

The Sydney architectural scene was influenced by the major international figures of the first modern generation. Nevertheless, even opposed tendencies showed a common concern to integrate features of the local landscape into domestic architecture, as well as a broad move to define and to create a 'regional' architecture. Sydney felt a renewed affinity with California,[4] whose climate, landscape and lifestyle seemed so similar to its own. A number of architects borrowed ideas and details for their houses from Californian magazines. L.A. architect Gordon Drake was much admired by Bill Lucas and Russell Jack, two of the Sydney architects whom Murcutt knew in the late 1950s. Drake's domestic architecture reflected the influence of Japan, where he was based during the war; it was also rooted in the geography, climate and raw materials of California. Drake emphasized the architect's responsibility to take account of place and social needs.[5]

The modern movement also reached Sydney through work being done in Scandinavia. There, too, modernism had been both tempered and enriched by the strong native traditions in the vernacular buildings and its close relationship with the landscape and local craftsmanship. Travel to Finland and the discovery of Aalto's work proved important for young Sydney architects, such as Ken Woolley and Keith Cottier, both of whom Murcutt knew in his student years.[6] The affinities between Australia and Scandinavia were reinforced when the Danish architect Jørn Utzon won the competition for the Sydney Opera House in 1957. Utzon, whose dramatic scheme celebrated the poetic force of Sydney's harbour, was a charismatic figure in local architectural circles during his four years in Australia.

Mies van der Rohe
Farnsworth House
Opening pages of an article in
Architectural Forum, October 1951

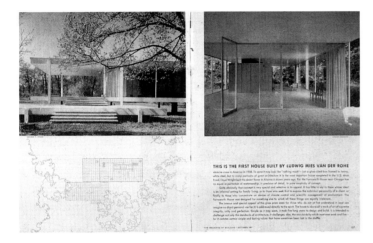

THIS IS THE FIRST HOUSE BUILT BY LUDWIG MIES VAN DER ROHE

FORMATIVE YEARS

Murcutt was familiar with architecture and building from his youth. His father, Arthur Murcutt, quit gold prospecting in New Guinea to work as a builder and developer in Sydney, where he also ran a small joinery business. A believer in the 'economy of survival' and a disciple of the American writer Henry David Thoreau's spartan and individualist philosophy, he had a keen interest in new forms of architecture and subscribed to several American periodicals, including *Architectural Forum*. There, in 1951, the young Glenn saw Mies van der Rohe's Farnsworth house,[7] which he carefully studied. Its seminal image was to reassert itself periodically in his work with the persistent regularity of a childhood memory. Using the design vocabulary of the imported architectural journals, Arthur Murcutt – an impenitent do-it-yourself man – built a number of houses on sites he had bought on the northern shores of the harbour. He prefabricated joinery in his workshop, made large timber façade panels, and developed simple but ingenious roof-ventilation systems and swimming-pool filters. Murcutt is also indebted to his father for his early introduction to the large wood-and-corrugated-iron agricultural sheds of the Sydney region, as well as to the houses of Frank Lloyd Wright, Charles Eames and Sydney Ancher, one of the early Australian post-war modernists.

When he began to study architecture in 1956, Glenn Murcutt soon developed an interest in the work of the Californian architects, above all Richard Neutra and Craig Ellwood. The appeal they held for him elucidates several central themes in his work in the years to come. He eagerly read Neutra's recently published *Mystery and Realities of the Site*, which advanced the case for a sensitive unity of architecture and place, supporting his argument with his own work. In his houses Neutra increasingly departed from the strict canons of modern architecture that he himself had helped introduce to California. According to the context, he used brick, timber and brise-soleils on long lightweight pavilions. He situated some of his buildings amidst light-reflecting pools, which served to cool the surroundings, store water and even provide irrigation.

Ellwood, who was thirty years younger than Neutra, found inspiration in Japanese architecture. Using industrial techniques and standard components, he transposed elements of Mies's buildings, alloying the American tradition of construction catalogues to the aesthetics of International Style. His training as an engineer and quantity surveyor had given him rigour and constructive deftness with a taste for standardized details. He designed three acclaimed houses for the Case Study Houses program, in which Neutra also participated, as did a rising generation of architects, Charles and Ray Eames and Pierre Koenig.

The Case Study Houses program, launched in 1945 by *Arts and Architecture*, had a pronounced impact and largely rehabilitated the social issue of innovative private houses that enhanced the Californian lifestyle. Its aim was to build up a coherent collection of model houses that subsumed the architect's personality. The proposed program was simple and realistic: the design was economical and suitable for mass production, the techniques innovative and standard. The conception and realization of each prototype was followed step by step, from issue to issue, like a scientific experiment. The sponsoring manufacturers and the products used were systematically named and described. Once finished, each house was opened to public inspection. Reyner Banham suggests that 'Murcutt got remarkably close to the California Case Study House style, even before he had visited California or met Craig Ellwood'.[8] As Esther McCoy observed, the CHS proved that 'small practices could contribute significantly to the writing of a new chapter in the history of the small house'.[9] While particularly applicable to Murcutt's career, this comment is also relevant to Australia as a whole, because domestic architecture is virtually the only field in which buildings of quality are now produced.

Between 1956 and 1962, while still a student, Murcutt came across a number of influential figures of the so-called Sydney School: Neville Gruzman and Russell Jack, for both of whom he worked, and Wilfred (Bill) Lucas – all architects of very different character. With these men he gained his first professional experience, coming up against their ideals and models and expanding his vicarious acquaintance with the European and American buildings he would later visit.

The term 'school' implies that there was a homogenous architectural movement subscribing to a common tendency in Sydney at the time. In reality Sydney School architects had mixed allegiances, ranging from Wright to Aalto to late Le Corbusier as interpreted by British neo-Brutalism. In their disparate fashions they none the less represented a romantic, regional approach to domestic architecture; they advocated the integration of a house to a site's contours and indigenous vegetation rather than its suburban setting, and the use of crude, even expressionist, natural materials. These principles enabled them to respond to the steep, wooded sites scattered with rocks previously regarded as impossible to build on but today carved up into plots throughout the northern areas of Sydney, and to circumvent the shortage of sophisticated manufactured materials and of skilled craftsmen in Australia at the period.

The architecture of Neville Gruzman, with whom Murcutt worked on two occasions, was inventive and disciplined in its detailing. Initially influenced by European modernism, he was a forerunner in the use of a standard curtain wall composed of aluminium sections and glazed panels, which he used as the exterior walls of an apartment building. An ensuing period of study in Japan, reinforced by his growing interest in Wright from 1955, gave his work a more organic character. Gruzman then moved towards a more introverted style, exemplified by the Probert house, whose opaque brickwork façades resolutely turn away from the road; inside the enclosing walls, living rooms and small internal courtyards are linked by large sliding-glass doors.

At that time Gruzman shared an office with Bill and Ruth Lucas, who were building their own house at Castlecrag, later dubbed The Glass House. They had wanted a minimal, economic dwelling that was suited to the climate and did not alter the natural site. The house consisted of a cut-out platform perched above the trees, supported by a thin frame of rough-sawn hardwood and steel, enclosed by glazed panels of various types and roofed in corrugated asbestos cement. The provocative idealism and radical form of this attempt at total

Neville Gruzman
Montrose Apartments
North Sydney, 1954
Photo: Max Dupain

Neville Gruzman
Probert House
Sydney, 1957–58
Photo: Max Dupain

communion with the environment ('the best architecture is no architecture')[10] rapidly turned the Lucas house into a cult object for an entire generation of Sydney architects.

Murcutt also worked as an assistant at the firm Allen & Jack; Russell Jack was his former teacher. An early follower of Wright, he was also interested in the traditional architecture of Japan and Scandinavia and the Californian work that showed the influence of these countries, such as Ellwood's. This is evidenced in the composite vocabulary of his houses, where a post-and-beam structure is combined with long planes of brickwork.

In the meantime Murcutt had graduated as an architect. His final thesis[11] contained two revealing epigraphs: one from Neutra, urging the spirit of the place to cooperate with the architect; the other from Le Corbusier's *Concerning Town Planning* – 'only the architect can create a balance between man and his environment'. Murcutt studied the housing schemes of Jørn Utzon in Denmark, traditional Greek villages and garden cities. He also examined the possibilities of a dense but humane alternative to the proliferation of one-family houses in Australian developments.

Concurrently, he built his first house, for the Olympic swimming champion John Devitt. Blind brick screens on the street side create privacy, while a long glazed façade extends from a covered atrium beneath a brise-soleil on the garden side. The contrast between the two façades, reminiscent of Gruzman and Jack, as well as Neutra, introduces a recurrent theme in Murcutt's work: the contrary treatment of the two main façades according to their orientation.

In 1962 Murcutt moved temporarily from Sydney to London. He worked at Frazer & Associates for two years and travelled in Europe, visiting the works of Dudok, Rietvelt and, above all, Le Corbusier. The high points of his first foreign tour proved to be the Mediterranean and Scandinavia. In Greece he was fascinated by the geometric forms of the whitewashed village houses of the Cyclades viewed in a clear and intense maritime light that reminded him of Australia's. In Denmark he was able to see Utzon's housing; in Sweden the Woodlands and Gävle crematoriums. He discovered Alvar Aalto's work in Finland and remained lastingly impressed by

Bill and Ruth Lucas
Lucas House
Castlecrag, Sydney, 1957
Photo: David Moore

Glenn Murcutt
Devitt House
1960–62, appearing in *Sydney Morning Herald*, 16 February 1964

the role of nature and the landscape in the creation of architectural order in all his buildings. 'Finland is the home of modern architecture', he wrote enthusiastically to his parents in Australia.[12]

On his return to Sydney Murcutt entered the competition for Espoo new town near Helsinki.[13] He then took a job as project architect with Ancher, Mortlock, Murray & Woolley, where he established a close, almost filial, relationship with Sydney Ancher, although not directly working with him. Ancher had travelled in Europe in the early days of Modernism, few innovations of which had reached Australia. He had been impressed by the house that Mies presented at the 1931 Berlin Bauhaus Exhibition.[14] While fairly conventional in their plans, Ancher's houses borrowed from the International Style its white boxes with flat roofs and glass walls, but also from domestic Australian architecture, reinterpreting its pergolas and verandas in a spare manner. Ancher was famous for winning the battle of the 'new aesthetic' in the late 1940s against Sydney's municipal authorities, who refused to give planning permission for a house with a roof terrace. Ancher's own house in Coffs Harbour, NSW, built in 1968, did much to revive the use of corrugated iron as roofing.[15]

With Ken Woolley, Murcutt worked on many large-scale projects, including new university buildings on the Newcastle campus,[16] where they both gave free rein to their passion for Finnish architecture. He simultaneously produced several designs for his mother's house (which was not built), definitively breaking away from the romantics of the Sydney School and allying himself with the international modernists. In 1969 he left Ancher, Mortlock, Murray & Woolley and set up his own practice.

As with so many of his mentors, it was with his own house that Murcutt was at last able to give form to his ideas. Although modest in scale and ambition, his Wunda Road renovation is significant in a number of respects. First, its obvious Miesian affiliation links the project to Californian or Scandinavian architecture of similar provenance. Second, its main design principle – the unification of part of the interior by removing dividing walls in the living areas and the gradual opening to the garden in linear sequence – introduces one

of his favourite themes. Last, the project won him the 1972 Gray and Mulroney Award of the Royal Australian Institute of Architects. The award was funded by two estate agents who wanted to reward architectural excellence for alterations to existing buildings that improved the country's heritage. The prize was a round-the-world airplane ticket for a study tour.

Murcutt then travelled in late 1973 to Mexico, the United States – a long-standing ambition – and Europe. In Los Angeles he at last met Ellwood, the Californian embodiment of his Miesian references, and visited his Rosen and Daphne houses, the latter of which would be recalled in the layout of his Ockens house four years later. In Barcelona, Murcutt met José Antonio Coderch, whose humanism, even more than his architecture, made a profound impression on him. Most significantly, he saw Pierre Chareau's Maison de Verre in Paris, which had a decisive influence. The Marie Short house in Kempsey, realized on his return, shows that he had already assembled most of his architectural vocabulary by this early stage.

Of Murcutt's exchanges with Australian architects of his own generation, the most significant was (and still is) with Richard Leplastrier, heir to the same architectural tradition of lightweight buildings that were permeable to the environment. He, too, was drawn to minimal dwelling and the single-cell house, and fascinated by the way architecture could reveal the genius of the place by the study of natural structures, by sailing and by craft. However, the source of Leplastrier's influences can also be found in the work of Utzon, with whom he worked in Sydney when the Opera House was under construction, and in Japan, where he later went for a long period of study.[17] Murcutt and Leplastrier taught together at the University of Sydney while they were building the farmhouse at Kempsey and the Palm House in Sydney, respectively. They also visited each other's building sites.

In the Palm House, Leplastrier experimented with materials, forms and, most importantly, with functional and spatial distribution, traces of which can be found in Murcutt's later work. The house backs on to a thick, rammed earth boundary wall. This wall acts as a spine containing all the wet areas, which open like cupboards onto

Pierre Koenig
Case Study House
Los Angeles, 1958

Craig Ellwood
Kubly House
Pasadena, Los Angeles, 1964–65
Photo: Brigitte Donnadieu

Glenn Murcutt
Murcutt House
Wunda Road, Mosman, Sydney, 1969
Photo: Frank Gardner Color Prints

the longitudinal corridor. Two principal garden-oriented rooms, both bounded by light metal frames, are grafted on to this 'service spine'. The boundaries between inside and outside can be dissolved at will with sliding panels and canvas diaphragms – a feature inspired by Leplastrier's experience in yacht building. The barrel-vaulted roof of the living rooms is made of corrugated copper; the central double gutter forms the ceiling of the corridor. The Palm House is a precious object, a splendid curiosity. Its design principle visibly inspired Murcutt in the Nicholas house, built immediately after the Kempsey farmhouse, which contains a 'serving-served' partition under parallel but asymmetrical roofs. Leplastrier's Palm House found a sort of counterpart in Murcutt's Bingi Point summer house ten years later.

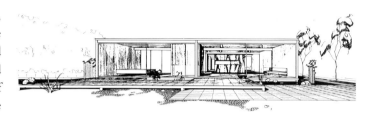

Murcutt's travels and experiences have constantly nourished the evolution of his architecture. After his meeting with Luis Barragán in Mexico in 1986, fountains and solid coloured walls enriched his buildings, seen to effect in the Mining Museum in Broken Hill and in urban projects such as the Magney house in Paddington. Murcutt's professed empathy for characteristic Aboriginal concepts of land and culture has now become a tangible inspiration, apparent in recent architectural projects he has made with the participation of certain communities in the Northern Territory. His oeuvre rests essentially, however, on the interaction of three main references, milestones of his maturation and constant stimulators of his designs: European modernism through Mies van der Rohe and Chareau, the functionalist tradition of Australian agricultural and industrial buildings, and the natural world and its expression in the local landscape.

MIES AND CHAREAU

Murcutt singles out two monuments of twentieth-century domestic architecture that had a decisive impact on his development: the 1950 Farnsworth house by Mies van der Rohe and the 1931 Dalsace house ('Maison de Verre') by Pierre Chareau and Bernard Bijvoët. Everything seems to set these two icons of modern architecture in opposition to each other. The Farnsworth house, pure, transparent,

Richard Leplastrier
Palm House
Sydney, 1973–75. Cross section and plan
Photos: Kate Wimble

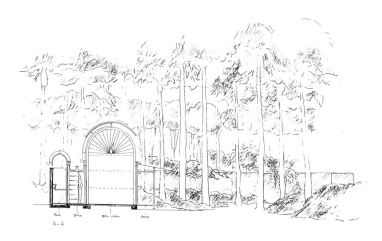

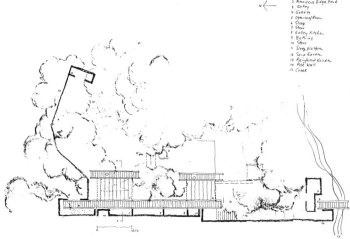

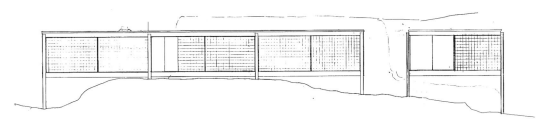

isolated in an untouched nature, 'rewards aesthetic contemplation before it fulfills domestic necessity',[18] a manifestation of classical thought aspiring to the timelessness of the temples. On the other hand, the Maison de Verre, functional beyond the bounds of strict necessity, is the ultimate machine to live in, an enclosed world born of the encounter between a highly restricted urban situation and an architect 'bricoleur avant le déluge'.[19]

Logically enough, the two houses play contradictory and complementary roles for Murcutt. The Farnsworth house, which he has never seen at first hand,[20] remains a basic image, the origin of his allegiance to Mies, a clue to his architectural vocabulary. His discovery of the Maison de Verre coincided with a visit there in 1973.[21] To this day Murcutt describes the revelation of Chareau's extraordinary world as a liberating experience, confirmation that 'modernity without dogma' was at last possible. The dual influence of Mies and Chareau explains the two poles spanned by his oeuvre: the reference to a universal model of architecture and a rational, poetic, do-it-yourself approach.

The influence of Mies explains a central part of Murcutt's design philosophy. Murcutt wholeheartedly adheres to the well-known principles 'less is more' and 'almost nothing'. He attributes great importance to a process of patient refinement by which these ideals are achievable, espousing another Miesian principle: 'Form is not the aim of our work, but only the result'.[22] On every scale, down to the last detail of the structure, his successive preliminary sketches reveal the quest for a plan purged of its dross – 'the three-quarters, not six-eighths solution', as he put it – and the methodical progression from the jumble of requirements dashed off on paper to their expression in a pacified and legible order. 'I see simplicity not so much as a disregard for complexity but as the clarification of the significant,' he wrote in 1980.[23]

Murcutt not only subscribes to Mies's ideas; he also repeats some of his forms. His first houses in the early 1970s sometimes borrowed literally from Mies's work. Some of his sketches for the Daphne-Murcutt house were indeed exercises 'in the manner of'; when renovating his own home in Wunda Road, Murcutt grafted an ex-

plicitly Miesian motif onto the back of the existing brick bungalow. The plan of the house Murcutt designed for his brother Douglas is partly derived from the Farnsworth house: the living room is divided by a central 'service' block. The accommodation opens onto a little courtyard on one side and a garden on the other, all of which is surrounded by a continuous brick wall reminiscent of Mies's 1930s ideal courtyard houses. The off-centre columns are yet another echo of the Farnsworth house; the simple timber frame and the entirely glazed northern façade of large sliding-glass doors display a kinship with some of Sydney Ancher's most Miesian houses. In the Laurie Short house Murcutt wrapped the dining area within a curved partition wall, a fleeting allusion to Mies's Tugendhat house, which had already appeared in the preliminary sketches of some of Murcutt's earlier houses. In its clear definition and handling of the corner I-beam sections, the black steel frame is related to Mies's great American buildings, but the static look of the Short house, heavily anchored to the ground, brings it closer to the work of Philip Johnson than Mies's and the highly partitioned interior lacks the fluidity of the Miesian plan.

Murcutt returned to the Farnsworth house for inspiration in 1974, when he designed the Marie Short house at Kempsey, the model for his farmhouses. Like Ellwood's Kubly house, it is an interpretation of Mies's design in wood. On the inside face of the off-centred, load-bearing columns, Murcutt attached a suspended wooden floor, a response to the threat of flooding that had similarly faced Mies: in protecting the Farnsworth house from the waters of the Fox River he made it look like an altar detached from the earth. Each of Murcutt's twin naves ends in a veranda open on three sides and contained by a simple prolongation of the horizontal plan. The spatial organization of the residential pavilion makes explicit reference to the single-cell plan so dear to Mies.

The image of the Farnsworth house persists in filigree in many of Murcutt's subsequent projects, though progressively diluted by his own increasingly idiosyncratic language. Specific evocations of Mies continue to reassert themselves, sometimes unexpectedly, as the suspended floors linked by a metal staircase in the Magney

**Glenn Murcutt
Laurie Short House**
Terrey Hills, Sydney, 1972–73
Photo: Max Dupain

**Glenn Murcutt
Marie Short House**
Kempsey, New South Wales, 1974–75
Photo: Max Dupain

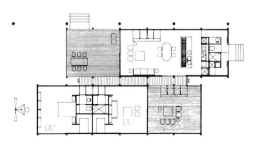

house at Paddington. Above all, the Farnsworth house remains one of the enduring emblems of Murcutt's basic design: the long glass pavilion mediating between Man and Nature.

In counterpoint to his manifest allusions to Mies, Murcutt's discovery of Chareau has left a less obvious trace on his architecture, but reveals a more intuitive affinity with Chareau's technique. In its reconciliation of the seemingly contradictory possibilities of industry and craft, the Maison de Verre acted as the catalyst of a significant shift in Murcutt's work.

Well before 1973 Murcutt had contemplated using mass-produced components in his buildings. The idea was already widespread: Eames and Ellwood had both designed houses as refined industrial objects. After leaving the firm of Ancher, Mortlock, Murray & Woolley to practice on his own, Murcutt had collected the catalogues of a range of manufacturers, particularly those specializing in metal sections. He had also planned to convert a large agricultural shed owned by his family by assembling standard clip-on components. At the same time he pursued a parallel interest in the age-old skills of traditional craft, as well as its rhythms and materials. In Sydney he had worked for a long time in his father's business with a master joiner, Bill Davidson. In Finland he had been captivated by the thriving role of craft and the individualization of architect-designed details, particularly Aalto's.

One aspect of the Maison de Verre clearly suggested to Murcutt a brilliant response to the dilemma of fusing industry and craftsmanship: by employing his metal-joiner Dalbet to adapt a number of mass-produced components, Chareau daringly and skilfully combined industrial products with the craftsman's expertise. Inverting the principle of standardization, he turned mass-produced parts into unique elements, effectively transmuting the ordinary into the extraordinary and raising the finished object to the status of a *chef d'œuvre* without sacrificing its modern character.

This discovery had an important effect on Murcutt's work, strikingly apparent in his buildings immediately after 1973. He suddenly moved away from the somewhat rigid modernism of his earlier houses and renewed contact with the tradition of Australian architecture well suited to his growing preoccupation with climate-conditioned design solutions. Comparison of the first design for the Cullen house in Sydney and the final building, respectively dated 1972 and 1974, provides an apt example. But it is above all in his isolated country houses, in Kempsey and Mount Irvine, that Murcutt began to celebrate materials – revealing curved metal roofs, playing with the grain and colour of the timber structure and cladding. By using standard parts in an increasingly systematic and individual manner, without basing the aesthetics of the house on a display of industrial origins – but without negating them either – he was able to exploit his knowledge of construction catalogues.

Apart from two brief forays into the field of project housing, Murcutt has shown little interest in mass-produced construction. Even when designed and built on 'invariant' principles and using a recurrent range of materials, each of his houses is a prototype without a successor. He nevertheless rarely has recourse to custom-made parts. His firm belief in industry and a concern for cost lead him to opt for the available ready-made products and to adapt them if necessary. When using the components unaltered, he achieves his desired effect by the ingenuity and elegance with which he assembles them. When modifying them, he does so like a tailor adjusting a semi-tailored suit. In project after project he has transformed standard fireplaces, doors (which he has converted into external sliding doors and panels, and enlarged by fitting wind-braces). He modified the metal purlins commonly used to build garden huts in the design of the Carey house. The design process and a vision of the possible outcome, which never cease to be adjusted one to the other and mutually enriched, are thus of equal importance in the final achievement.

For the 1974 Kempsey farmhouse Murcutt developed a façade based on traditional features of Australian buildings. The system consists of three superimposed layers: sets of louvres juxtaposed between load-bearing elements, panels of fine metal insect mesh, and wooden or aluminium venetian blinds. The louvres, made of steel or glass according to the orientation and function of the internal space, are standard components – the steel version is in fact reminis-

cent of the 'gills' Chareau designed for the living room in the
Maison de Verre. The façade, the full length of which is mobile, can
be tuned to different conditions or provide the different filtrations
assigned to the outer wall, becoming thereby an 'active skin', to
borrow Richard Rogers's felicitous term for Chareau's façade.[24]

The Maison de Verre is indeed distinguished by an 'ideology of
mobility', as Kenneth Frampton has observed: the owners are able
to adapt the building to their changing requirements by adjusting
specific features that affect the very nature of the internal space.
This clearly encouraged Murcutt to conceive his houses as climatic
machines, using selected mass-produced parts to make the façade
adjustable. Apart from enabling the inhabitant to maintain as closely
as possible the same conditions inside as outside, if so wished, the
flexibility of the Kempsey façade allows the intensity of light to be
regulated and to determine the intimacy of particular areas. Murcutt
designs his buildings as simple devices that the user can work like a
sailboat or tune like a musical instrument. The electrically operated
venetian blinds laid horizontally on the roof of the Done house act
as diaphragms and turn its verandas and gallery into light traps. The
pivoting façade of the Marika house can function equally as wall or
awning and allows for endless combinations of the two.

Another instance of Murcutt's affinity with Chareau lies in the
way Murcutt makes use of practical functions to express the architectural effect of sequence, form or texture. To ventilate the mining
museum in Broken Hill, for example, Murcutt 'mechanized' a system of wind traps – the Middle Eastern *malqaf* – by introducing an
anemometer linked to a mobile flap which automatically modulates
the influx of air to the wind velocity. He sized each *malqaf* to suit the
needs of the building, reinterpreted its traditional form, and gave
the façade some of its sculptural force by the repetition of the created element. Murcutt also designed a rainwater head by assembling
a fine steel sheet folded to make a flange and an ordinary steel downpipe. The resulting element fulfills a threefold role: it creates an efficient funnel, expresses the whirling flow of water, and becomes an
architectonic feature, akin to a column. Murcutt thus isolates essential or ordinary functions and turns them into poetic objects.

However, two recent projects illustrate Murcutt's sometimes ambivalent attitude toward the expression of function and the mingling of craft techniques with industrial aesthetics. In the Pratt house Murcutt did not make a feature of the above. On the contrary: the controls of the large pivoting glass panels were encased inside triangular boxes; the metal skeleton of the building, an elaborate combination of commercially manufactured sections, was purged of factory marks and welding seams. Here, the mechanisms of the building are concealed, from the steel-maker's trademarks to any traces of assembly techniques. Murcutt thus achieved a 'cast' metal frame with a perfectly smooth finish. (Mies is said to have had a similar objective with the steel sections of the Farnsworth house, which he insisted be polished almost into abstraction.) As the Pratt house was nearing completion, Murcutt built the Kempsey studio out of a small existing shed. Using second-hand wood as an adjunct to new material, Murcutt carefully chose to distinguish between old and new to contrast their specific qualities – 'à la Scarpa', as he put it. He tailored the design to the available cross-sections, the timber's characteristics and his own express desire to minimize waste. Turning economic constraints into a functional and aesthetic exercise, he took advantage of traces from the reclaimed material's previous uses: an old bolt-hole, for example, became the drip on an external beam when its end was obliquely cut off.

Thus, two distinct approaches interact and coexist in Murcutt's work. On the one hand he is the knowing architect, choosing and transforming materials to create the form he has in mind. On the other hand he is the do-it-yourself builder, the tinkerer who extracts the idea of a possible form from what happens to be available, celebrating the haphazard and making a virtue of necessity, combining heterogenous parts into a coherent whole. When he designed a studio for the American painter Robert Motherwell, Chareau, too, cobbled together disparate elements: the remains of a greenhouse and a Quonset Hut – a portable American army hut consisting of a light frame covered in corrugated iron sheets bent in a semicircle, many of which were converted into houses in the United States after the Second World War. Murcutt clearly had the

Glenn Murcutt
House
Opium Creek, Northern Territory,
1986. Preliminary sketch

Glenn Murcutt
Maestri House
Blueys Beach, New South Wales, 1981
Photos Andrew Payne

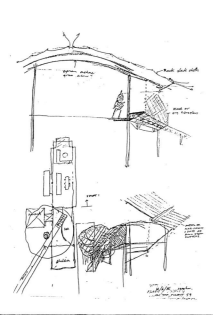

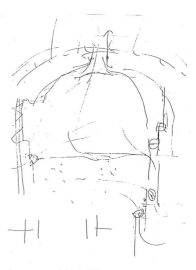

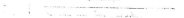

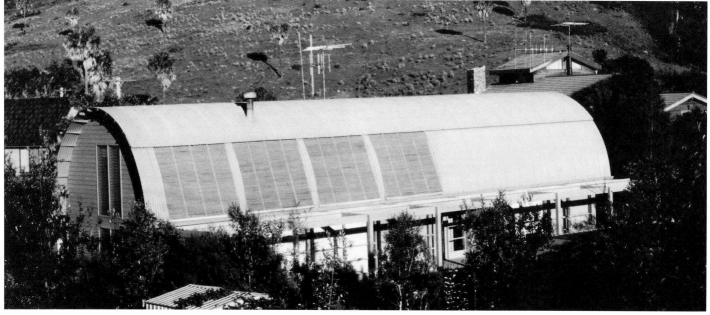

Jean Prouvé
Tropical House
1949. Preliminary sketches
Photo: J. C. Planchet, CC I, Centre Georges Pompidou

Glenn Murcutt
Maestri House
Blueys Beach, New South Wales, 1981
Photos Andrew Payne

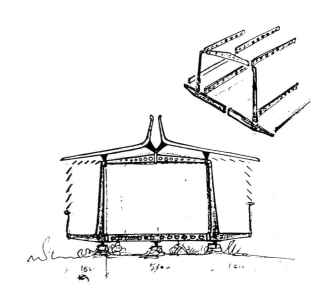

Motherwell studio in mind when he designed the Maestri house.

In the main, the influences of Murcutt's two mentors, Mies and Chareau, are played off against each other in his buildings; he uses one to critique the other. His minimalist spirit turns him away from what he sees as the pointless complexity of some of the mechanical devices – the 'bachelor machines' – in the Maison de Verre. Likewise Murcutt considers British High Tech – much influenced by Chareau – too formalist, indeed mannerist, and fails to share its adherents' fascination with the transfer of technologies. Inherited common sense equally leads him to turn away from the Farnsworth house's cold purity, its uninviting, almost hostile, perfection. The Kempsey house, his seminal work, is the key realization of a reconciled duality. While making explicit reference to the Miesian pavilion, Murcutt's model is softened by adaptation to the site, climate and local materials: the façades' integral 'triple skin', the corrugated iron roof, columnar drainpipes and their associated expressionism appear here simultaneously and for the first time.

Since then Murcutt has constantly juggled with the vocabulary of two complementary approaches to modern architecture. Let us point, for example, to Murcutt's 1986 sketch for a house in the Northern Territory: a long pavilion containing construction and climatic techniques akin to those of Murcutt's senior artisan engineer and 'metal twister', Jean Prouvé (who is also indebted to Chareau), in his 1949 prototype for a tropical house.

THE AUSTRALIAN TRADITION

In his quest for an architecture suited to its place, Murcutt inevitably turned to traditional Australian buildings. The only culture previous to European colonization was that of the Aborigines, an essentially nomadic people. Communities made their shelters out of limited natural resources, building temporary huts from branches covered with brushwood, leaves or large strips of bark. Murcutt, who began in the 1980s to document the structures of Aborigines,[25] believes that any resemblance between the form of their bark huts and his own buildings is explained by a similar sensitivity

to the same territory, not by the deliberate imitation on his part.

The buildings of the early European settlers, who lived in isolated rural or mining colonies, have occasionally been compared to some of these native dwellings. Using material from nearby forests, they are remarkable adaptations of the archetypal house. The frames are made from roughly squared tree trunks, the roofs from wide strips of bark taken from the trees then flattened, while the pieces laid over the ridge make use of the bark's natural curve to keep it watertight.

The history of the Australian house, however, is essentially a succession of styles imported from Britain and offered Murcutt few useful clues. The models were never fundamentally altered to take account of the specific Antipodean conditions, being only super-ficially acclimatized by the addition of awnings and verandas. Nine-teenth-century Australian houses did not differ substantially from the American cottages in Virginia at the same period. The veranda, a universal colonial feature favoured by the British since they took over India, was in no way particular to Australia. Murcutt retained the principle but not the traditional form of the veranda. It occurs in his buildings as an open area protected from sun and rain, a transitional social space between an often inhospitable outside world and the intimacy of the interior.

In parallel with the enduring models of the European house, a distinctive functionalist tradition developed in Australia. Farm and factory buildings, barns, warehouses, greenhouses and, above all, woolsheds and shearing sheds stand out in the vast expanses of the continent to this very day, testaments to the colonists' economic activities. In these examples Murcutt found an architecture that was specifically adapted to Australian context and free of aesthetic pre-conceptions: 'this appropriate architecture is clear, it is direct, it is obvious, it is logical, it is also beautiful',[26] he said of farms scattered in the bush and countryside.

These buildings and their 'aesthetics of necessity' have had a twofold impact on Murcutt's work. First, he borrows directly from them, adopting some of their techniques and materials when they answer an identical practical problem. The ventilation flaps between windows and walls in the Cullen and Magney houses, for example,

Experimental Farm Cottage
Parramatta, New South Wales, c. 1820.
A small colonial farm of the Georgian
period
Photo: Max Dupain

Agricultural Sheds
Kempsey region
Photos Glenn Murcutt

are derived from the little pivoting wooden shutters used to expel hot air from greenhouses. The composition of the façade in the Hillston farmhouse is inspired by a particular type of brick wool-shed ventilated by a wooden lattice directly below the curved roof. The Kempsey Museum's aluminium air extractors, both economical and efficient, are those commonly used in factory farming – a reminder of Murcutt's predilection for ordinary catalogue parts. Louvres, porous and adjustable, have become a basic component of Murcutt's 'climatic' façades. Similarly, Murcutt uses corrugated iron for the same practical reasons that led the pioneers to adopt it. Omnipresent in rural Australia, corrugated iron played an essential role in the colonization of the continental interior.[27] The introduction of corrugated galvanized iron after 1830, initially imported from Britain and manufactured in Australia from 1921, allowed easy and rapid building in the remotest parts of the island continent, which totally lacked infrastructures. Produced in stackable sheets, it was easy to transport, comparatively light and a ready complement to the widely available timber, which it quickly replaced as a roofing and boarding material. Bent, welded and bolted, corrugated iron was also used for cylindrical water tanks, necessary to the self-sufficiency of isolated bush farms. Murcutt regards it as the ideal material: adaptable, strong, cheap and light enough not to require a strong supporting frame. These qualities became invaluable when building in the untouched sites so highly prized for second homes.

Murcutt's use of supposedly 'basic' materials, chosen for their functional adaptability and incorporated into a perceptive body of work, makes him an altogether modern architect. He has dignified the use of corrugated iron and given it a role in contemporary architecture. In Kempsey and Glenorie, he employed it not only as roofing – as did a number of his contemporaries – but also as cladding. Murcutt thus makes the image of the museum or the house inseparable from that of the familiar and humble tin shed of the Australian countryside.

Murcutt strongly rejects, however, any suggestion that he is nostalgically reviving old rural images. The second aspect of his identification with Australian traditions is perhaps best described as

Glenn Murcutt with Peter Freeman
Project for 'Roeta' House
Hillston, New South Wales, 1989

Woolshed
Ghoolendaa-di, Boggabri, New South
Wales, *c.* 1890
Photo: Harry Sowden

Rail Sheds
Nuriootpa, South Australia, *c.* 1920
Photo: David Moore

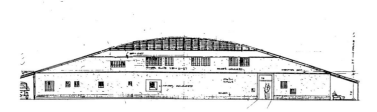

'analogous inspiration': applying the same logic that produced the farm buildings, he introduced a similar pragmatism into domestic architecture, inevitably effecting the reappearance of particular forms. By extending this approach to all aspects of his work, he has turned the tin shed – particularly the woolshed specific to Australia – into a paradigm.

While also derived from originally European models, the woolshed was by necessity quickly modified to its Australian geographical and climatic conditions. Geared to production, its architecture is calculated to operate efficiently. It is shaped to suit its function and internally divided into low stalls that reflect the organization of tasks. Its length is proportional to the scale of the enterprise, its height sufficient to allow hot air to rise and cool the interior by convection. The slope of the roof is calculated so that condensation runs laterally along its underside, following its corrugations without dripping inside the building. The floor is raised to avoid rising damp, to ventilate the building and to provide shelter underneath for the flock. The pavilions are coupled and linked at roof level by a flat box gutter whose widths are determined by the dimensions of standard iron sheets. Rain is collected and stored in metal tanks on the back of the building.[28]

From outside the oldest wooden woolsheds appear to have solid walls devoid of all openings. In reality adzed planks, or even whole limbs, are set into the shed's structural frames so that the dazzlingly intense sunlight, diminished by its passage through the interstices, penetrates the interior at a tolerable level. Judiciously sited in relation to the prevailing winds, the shed is also permanently aired through these slits. The building is thus lit and ventilated by its intrinsic design and construction.

The objective factors that have shaped the architecture of woolsheds describes an equivalent practical reasoning pursued by Murcutt and explains the resemblances between the sheds and a number of his houses, particularly the Kempsey and Jamberoo farmhouses: the siting of a building to take account of the direction of sun, wind and rain; post-and-beam construction using wood and corrugated iron, adapted to local materials and skills; the use of stilts

Glenn Murcutt
Fredericks House
Jamberoo, New South Wales, 1981–82
Photo: Max Dupain

Timber and Corrugated-Iron
Shearing Shed
Lake Mungo, Menindee, New South
Wales, 1869. The structure in
the landscape, with interior and
exterior views
Photo: Françoise Fromonot

Glenn Murcutt
Kempsey Museum
New South Wales, 1976–82
Photo: Glenn Murcutt

'Make Do'
Revolving cabinet made from a 44-gallon
metal drum fitted with drawers, *c.* 1925
*Photo: Penelope Clay, Powerhouse
Museum, Sydney*

to protect from flooding; walls that are permeable to air and light (with the resulting striations of light); and the clear linear progression of different but interlinked spaces within the outer envelope. In similarly wild and open territory Murcutt has also produced, albeit on a different scale, the same linear response as the woolsheds to the horizontality that in his eyes typifies the Australian landscape, but this has not deterred him from introducing the outline of the woolshed to houses in the heart of Sydney.

The coincidence between an old building type intended for agricultural use and a contemporary house may seem paradoxical. It is made possible, as Reyner Banham has observed, by the ambiguity implicit in the functional specificity of the woolsheds and their character: 'long, abstract sheds . . . as generic as medieval barns . . . their long clear-span interiors make them ideal receptacles for almost any other bunch of functions'.[29]

Practical improvisation on one hand, a persistent model on the other: Murcutt's connection to tradition and to modernity are in symmetry with each other. But his applications do not reduce themselves to a simple parallelism, and his two reference sources reveal unexpected similarities.

In sum, Murcutt's synthesis of the Farnsworth house and the Australian woolshed merges these two images by drawing on their kinships. Ludwig Glaeser and Philip Johnson have identified an important source of Mies's architecture[30] in the anonymous industrial buildings of late-nineteenth-century Germany, and hence in the *Fachwerkbauten*, the earlier traditional form of timber construction of which they are the steel version. The Kempsey house is thus a local form of the Farnsworth house's distant forebears. On the other hand, the old practice of 'do-it-yourself', the so-called 'make do', occupies a category of its own in Australian popular art. This pioneer tradition has produced many ingenious examples of everyday objects made out of ordinary or reclaimed material. Manufactured goods have been altered from their original form and shaped for a variety of purposes, agricultural and domestic. For example, simple metal drums have been turned into astonishing movable cupboards with pivoting drawers, inspired by those featured in early-twentieth-century household-equipment catalogues. It is tempting to draw an unexpected parallel with the devices that Eileen Grey or Chareau introduced into some of their furniture.

Thus the recognition of indirect echoes of his country's own traditions in the work of Mies and Chareau may have helped bring about Murcutt's return to the vernacular. It seems that through the medium of his two modern masters he was brought back circuitously to the sensibility and forms that had always surrounded him. His interest in vernacular traditions stems above all from his penchant for simple, rational, commonsense solutions, which is linked to his search for an architecture founded on a basic notion of the human dwelling – the peasant's house in the Black Forest described by Heidegger to illustrate his famous etymological connection between living, building and being. For Murcutt this deep affinity with tradition is also, however, a recognition of a timeless and universal knowledge of nature and the respect for its laws.

NATURE AND LANDSCAPE

Murcutt's education developed in him a questing cast of mind, ever striving to understand the processes that lead to forms, while rationalist logic has helped him to extract crucial generative concepts from these reflective processes. He has always been interested in biology, botany and geology, and his observations of life systems and their mechanisms produce analogical pretexts that nourish his architecture. Murcutt's phenomenological analysis of the landscape is therefore critical to his 'interpretation in built form'.[31]

Australia's privileged relationship with the natural world is deeply inscribed in the still-recent history that links the continent to Western spheres. The principal aim of British expeditions to the South Pacific at the end of the eighteenth century was to chart the last unexplored regions of the globe and to complete human knowledge of nature. Cook's voyages, which led to the annexation by the British Crown of the austral continent, then known as New Holland, were first and foremost scientific missions. Naturalists, botanists and draftsmen accompanied Cook in order to describe, name and classi-

fy the animals, plants and native people. Australia, the gigantic island isolated very early on from the rest of the world by continental drift, offered to European investigation a population of 'savages' presumed to be 'untouched' (it was later claimed that they were a forty-thousand year old survival of the Stone Age), as well as preserved, distinctive flora and fauna. Cook and Joseph Banks christened the first place they explored in the environs of what was to become Sydney, Botany Bay. Inspired by the underlying universalist principles of the Enlightenment, the discoveries borne out of these explorations of new horizons and specimens later provided Darwin with the critical evidence to support his theory of evolution. Reported throughout Europe, the findings influenced landscape painting and nurtured the nascent romantic taste for scientific precision in representations of the picturesque.[32]

From its foundation in 1788 as a penitentiary colony on the shores of the harbour, Sydney was associated with nature, whose redemptive virtues, it was believed, could improve humankind. The ensuing colonization brought the Europeans into constant confrontation with an untainted and unknown environment. A renewed awareness of the city's remarkable location and the role it had to play in design was an important development for the architects with whom Murcutt studied in the late 1950s; it was also the period when Utzon began to build his Opera House. The magnificent coastal landscape had fired Utzon's inclination, partly inherited from Wright, for metaphors of nature to explain his choice of forms. His lyrical evocations remain famous: the clouds floating above the harbour headlands inspired the white-tiled shells on a sandstone platform, the wings of a sea bird the great articulated glass walls.

Murcutt recalls that Utzon's ideas confirmed his own tendency to refer to nature as the measure and ratio of artifacts. Early in his studies this predisposition had been reinforced by Noel Bazeley, who taught 'organic' construction. Murcutt recently acknowledged his lasting influence on his own thinking: 'We spent the entire first term . . . analysing continuity in nature . . . studying spider's webs, leaves, blades of grass, natural arched forms . . . We progressed in the second term to analysing continuity in constructed forms: bridges, vaults, cellular formations, foundations, reinforcing. We were learning how you design from nature. Things don't smash together, they transmute. There is a hierarchy of parts and a rational language in how the parts might fit together'.[33]

Though he soon broke away from the Wrightian leanings of some of his early student projects, Murcutt continued to attach an analysis of natural phenomena to the aesthetic implications – to ally the scientific with the picturesque. Nevertheless, his work does not mimic natural forms: for him beauty derives from the logical reply to a well-phrased question. Although he values the example and pedagogic virtues of nature, he does not retain its forms. Rather, he makes use of its lessons, drawing a series of parallels between the immutable principles that govern nature and those that should rule architecture.

The morphological modifications of a single plant species in relation to the terrain where it grows serves as a parable of the need to adapt architectural models to their environment. Although the farmhouses at Kempsey and Jamberoo are closely related and could almost be mistaken for each other, their façades and the position of their verandas have been adjusted to suit the climate of each place. The metamorphosis in a living organism's appearance according to the time of day or season suggests the idea of an adjustable house that is equipped to meet changing external conditions. The complexity and ambiguity of the phenomena occurring in the meeting of different elements – land and water, for example – underscore the importance of the 'betweenness', the veranda being an expression of this idea. The way living creatures fine down towards their extremities – antlers, eyelashes, wings, antennae – justifies the progressive thinning of a building towards its boundaries with the outside world, a sort of dematerialization that Murcutt calls 'feathering', by which the building 'peels' away towards its peripheries. In the Pratt house, the awnings are constructed from half-cantilevered, graduated tinted-glass 'scales', so that the illusion of their lightness is heightened. In the Ball house, the platform slats on the edge of the veranda are set further apart to progressively reveal the forest floor; on the edge of the ceiling the plasterboard stops short, the metal frame is exposed,

and the purlins are pared down so that only the thickness of the metal sheet meets the sky. Analyzing the size of living structures' parts – in a foot or a wing – in relation to their role, Murcutt strictly dimensions the elements of a building's skeleton so that it precisely expresses the forces to which it is subject. In his steel structural frames he often designs a cruciform section with flanges larger at the base, thus reflecting their actual increasing loads. He is also interested in the pursuit of efficiency, the economy of means developed in swimming and flying, their translation into navigation and aeronautics, and the logic of the resulting forms. By analogy, he requires an optimum return from his architectural effects, an ethic-aesthetic that meets – or explains – his minimalist approach.

Modifying an environment with the introduction of an extraneous object, which creates a new order while the object itself is altered by the existing order, has parallels in the construction of a new building on its site. Murcutt likes to cite the example of a brick thrown into a river that comes to a standstill once it has reached its *exact place* in the flow of currents and fresh turbulence created by its own presence. It is this relative equilibrium, the inevitable result of the interaction between objective forces, that he wants to achieve between a new building and its site.

This approach seeks to allow human intervention to insert itself into the assumed order of a place without contravening its laws. It is linked to the theories, familiar to Murcutt, of the American landscape architect Ian McHarg, who advocates the pragmatic use of ecology on a broad scale with the terrain. Knowledge of the natural characteristics of a place obtained by scientific analysis, he maintains, enables the architect to understand a site's possibilities, limitations and prohibitions so as to intervene in the most appropriate manner, while allowing him to step back to let the features shape the design.[34]

Murcutt explains his way of proceeding in similar terms. The regional geology, hydrography, climate and direction of the prevailing winds determine the house's positioning, its structure, and the greater or lesser porousness of the façades receiving the breezes necessary for ventilation. The sun's angle of incidence in different

Glenn Murcutt
Meagher House
Bowral, New South Wales, 1988–91.
Preliminary sketch for the glazing on the
north façade, which takes account of
seasonal changes in the angle of the
sun's rays

Glenn Murcutt
Marsh & Freedman Office
Redfern, Sydney, 1987–89. Cruciform
posts on the veranda facing the
courtyard
Photo: Glenn Murcutt

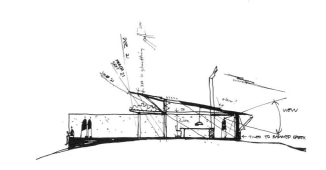

seasons determines the dimensions of the roof overhang, which cuts off the vertical rays of the sun in summer while the height of the façade's upper glazing allows the low winter sun to penetrate the heart of the interior. Openings and verandas are positioned in relation to the views and winds. The façade is thus a *result*, not an articulated formal composition by the architect. Lightweight (with juxtaposed glass panels) or opaque (with brick pierced by slits) it reveals little of the nature of the enclosed space from the exterior.

Murcutt draws from the landscape the conception of a building, thereby making it one of his design tools. He strives to formalize each site's characteristics to make them intelligible and perceptible and to transmit them to the dwelling's interior. When he says 'the landscape always informs us', he is indeed referring to the information it contains for the architect. But this is one of his fundamental assertions: architecture should remain in tune with the environment to ensure that the inhabitant is a part of the events around him. He seeks to communicate each site's physical and visual properties to the building's interior: the quality of light, winds, sounds, even scents – as in the museum in Broken Hill. In his town houses he retains only selected views for their closeness to nature, abstracting them as much as possible from manmade manifestations. In the house for his brother he grouped dwelling and garden within a high wall to form an almost fortified unit, open only to the sky, an ideal environment for the inhabitants, isolated from its ordinary suburban context. The Done house, though free from the constraints of party walls, is cut off from the street, practically blind on three sides, turned inwards around a patio and centred exclusively on the sea view. The Magney house belongs to a row of terrace houses in a relatively dense quarter of central Sydney, but Murcutt has calculated the height of the garden walls to create an illusion of isolation amidst the vegetation from the terrace. In each project Murcutt seeks a direct encounter with the landscape, true to his belief that nature manifests a superior order of positive value.

This conception of Nature – Man is one among other living creatures, an inseparable link in a chain that we must know, understand and respect – explains Murcutt's interest in traditional societies. He

admires the 'sensible relationship' that they have with their environment, their intimate knowledge of its resources and dangers. He spent his early childhood in New Guinea, at the time still an Australian colony. Having witnessed the war waged by the tribes on prospectors and settlers, he remembers the natives' informed and strategic use of a terrain that was indecipherable and hostile to the uninitiated. After the construction of the Kempsey museum, during which Murcutt had his first contacts with the Aborigines, he actively studied their way of life, which he sees as setting a precedent for the ideal symbiosis with the Australian continent.

The Europeans, who literally took the place of the original inhabitants, permanently altered a culture that had until then maintained a privileged dialogue and highly intense relationship with nature. Murcutt is fascinated by the millennial wisdom accumulated by various communities in order to survive in the difficult conditions of most regions of Australia. Their economic and spiritual activities made a noticeable impact on the indigenous landscape none the less: hunting grounds were cleared by burning and bark was stripped from trees for their huts, canoes and shields, though they never took more than they strictly needed. They engraved on rocks, carved on trees and raised totems, marking the territory with signs of ownership and their sacred customs through a 'land art' charged with ritual significance. Murcutt admires the ageless discernment with which they select and gather food and materials from the wild, respecting the finiteness of natural resources by necessity. He envies the discretion, the deeply ontological and symbolic character of their temporary shelters that incorporate their immediate surroundings and involve minimal architectural elaboration. For him, the Aboriginal culture emanates directly from the very place.

Thus Murcutt advocates an ecumenical conception of the Australian landscape, in his eyes the only common denominator of the immigrants that make up postwar Australia, almost an instrument of national reconciliation. Convinced by the teachings of nature and landscape that to be *appropriate* architecture must *respond to place,* he has made them absolute points of reference.

Part Two
Principles and Themes

THE ARCHITECT–ARTISAN

From the beginning, in 1970, Murcutt chose to practise architecture alone, without partners, regular assistants or even a secretary. He works from a house on Sydney's North Shore, using a simple drawing board, a telephone and a typewriter, supplemented recently by a fax and a word processor. One might add, as an ironical reply to critics who accuse him of repeating the same motifs, that he does not even have a photocopier. Most of his projects, including the hundreds of 'small jobs' – renovations, alterations, building extensions, mostly in and around Sydney – have been entirely designed and supervised by him alone, and he has at times managed close to thirty at a time.

Many architects in Australia have to work on a small scale, principally because of the way in which commissions are assigned. Competitions barely exist. Public and institutional projects, the domain of governmental architects and the few privileged firms who work with them, are virtually unobtainable by independent architects. Public housing, particularly of a collective kind, ceased to be a priority after the First World War. The bulk of private development programs logically fall to corporate firms with large resources, whose international style of production is conventional at best, but most mediocre. The house remains the cherished commission of Australian architects, inexhaustible manna in a country where most people dream of private property. Most small firms concentrate on domestic architecture, traditionally a catalogue of styles and influences, but also the laboratory of all tendencies and innovations.

This attitude is not, however, the only reason that Murcutt works as much as possible on his own. This fundamental commitment of working on his own is reminiscent of the deep-rooted pioneers' individualism, which he defends like an ethic and thereby radicalized a leaning latent in other Sydney architects. Richard Leplastrier, too, practises architecture at a pre-industrial level, on an almost family basis, in close and inspired dialogue with an enlightened client.

Murcutt has never wanted to take on the burden of a firm. It would cost him the freedom to travel and to accept invitations to teach abroad, notably in the United States. When necessary he will choose a young Sydney-based architect to produce drawings on his own premises or supervise a building site. Over the years he has periodically brought in former students, such as Alex Tzannes, Wendy Lewin, Graham Jahn and Reg Lark. His son Nicholas, also an architect, now assists him on specific projects. Murcutt is wary of established associations, which in his view inevitably lead to power struggles between the partners. If a site is too far from Sydney, he temporarily works with an associated local architect. With the extension of the Pratt house in Melbourne, for example, he was wholly responsible for the design, while a large local firm, Bates, Smart, McCutcheon, already engaged in the existing nineteenth-century building's restoration, prepared the working drawings and supervised the site work. Recently, he has moved towards a more conventional association, working with the Darwin firm Troppo as joint architects for the Landscape Interpretation Centre at Kakadu. In the near future, larger scale projects may force Murcutt into more frequent collaborations of this kind. Until now, however, he has for twenty-five years and with minimum delegation fulfilled his wish to carry the bulk of the work and responsibility himself.

Such a way of working may seem heroic, romantic, retrograde or avant-garde; it is in any event unusual. It reveals a personal conception of the architect's all-encompassing role, limits the quantity and nature of commissions Murcutt can handle, and partly explains the homogeneity of his oeuvre.

In every project Murcutt assumes responsibility for each decision taken, needing to justify it only to himself. A project's maturation involves continual readjustment of the concept to the design – and vice versa – until the optimum result is achieved. He subjects every decision to constant re-examination, refining and simplifying his plans, eliminating superfluity. That there is no division of labour makes it easier to achieve a synthesis of the disparate elements. Analysis, conception and design become physically indissociable, much like the working process of a craftsman. 'There is no doubt that our design instruments determine the forms we make,' he recently said.[35] Murcutt often quotes the words of Luis Barragán: 'Any work of architecture that does not express serenity is a mistake.' He goes on to add, 'working alone helps'.

This type of practice limits the number of commissions in progress at any one point. Murcutt seeks to control them to remain master of his own time, to protect his work from repetition of method. 'Since I am interested in people as individuals rather than anonymous consumers of architecture, much of my architecture is domestic in character . . . I have avoided major buildings by preference because in designing them one is isolated from the users.'[36] As a result he has concentrated almost entirely on houses, accepting rare projects of a public nature only if his relationship with the commissioning body satisfies him. He chooses his clients as much as they choose him, and some are even willing to wait several years for the next free space in his schedule. Now that his reputation affords him more choice, he only accepts commissions in which he is fully able to express his convictions in a fruitful relationship with like-minded clients. Who are they? Generally cultivated upper-middle class, they include lawyers, doctors, university professors and artists. There are exceptions, like an Aboriginal family (the pilot house), a young teacher (the cheapest house), and a wealthy entrepreneur (the most expensive house). The cost of each house is not generally made public, but Murcutt suggests a building cost of some $2000 per square metre, except when the client requests out-of-standard features.

Murcutt has likewise always sought to establish lasting, but empathetic and mutually exacting, relationships with the other professions involved in his projects. Since 1970 he has remained faithful to one family of structural engineers: first Dick Taylor, also a naval engineer, and now his son James. On several occasions he has paid tribute to their work, creativity and feeling for the 'architectural solution'.[37] Whenever possible he uses the same building firms, either directly appointing them or by limiting tendering work out to small family firms.

House plans generally take up three or four sheets of A2 paper. The first sheet contains the 1/100 drawings for building permission. In the working drawings Murcutt then executes a 1/20 transverse section, large-scale details of the main structural principles, and a series of variations on particular assembled parts. The drawing is spare, even diagrammatic, wholly free of affectation, with the emphasis on clarity and the quantity of information. The plans are covered in handwritten notes that often serve as specifications. Secondary elements and interior fixtures and fittings are dealt with in a later set of documents issued once building work has advanced enough. Murcutt has progressively rationalized particular elements – built-in kitchens and fireplaces, for example – so he can adapt his model from one house to another. Documentation is reduced to an efficient minimum. These concise graphic documents reflect the synthetic virtues of Murcutt's projects, their clarity and high degree of resolution. They testify to relationships with consultants and builders that are based on mutual respect and shared knowledge of construction.

ARCHITECTURAL TYPOLOGY

Murcutt sometimes speaks of the 'chess game of design'. The metaphor is clear: in architecture, the object, rules and pieces are prescribed; each new game presupposes a fresh strategy applied in a sequence of logical decisions. Making his own synthesis of influences, Murcutt began to assemble the groundwork for his methods and principles as far back as 1974: the Kempsey house crystallized his thoughts on modern and traditional architecture and the adaptation of buildings to climate and landscape. Thereafter, he ceaselessly juggled with the same preoccupations in relation to the constraints of each new site, each new project, each new client. He thus constructed a series of singular projects from which there emerge a recurrent vocabulary and grammar – one could almost speak of *characters*, by analogy with those identified through the observation of a group of specimens in order to define them as a species.

Murcutt's buildings follow a rectangular plan, long and lean, very rarely inflected. The genealogy of this form can be traced to the two founding models of his architecture: the Miesian pavilion and

**Variations on the
Elongated Plan**
Ball-Eastaway House, Glenorie (in the
forest); Magney House, Bingi (on the
coast); Muston House, Seaforth (in the
suburbs); Marika House, Eastern
Arnhem Land (in a tropical climate)

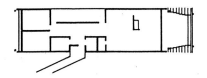

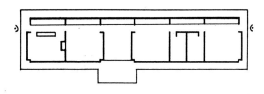

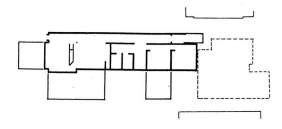

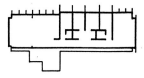

the Australian woolshed. This form reflects the constructive logic of the post-and-beam system in most of Murcutt's work; his elongated buildings are therefore no more than one room wide, allowing natural cross-ventilation. Yet the rectangular plan is not simply a formal pretext: Murcutt's preliminary drawings show the patient, methodical stages of the ordering by which the form was reached.[38] In his houses and his few larger buildings, whatever the site and climate, Murcutt always ends up with a linear interlinking of internal areas that represent a succession of functions and offer longitudinal passage from end to end.

Murcutt's very first projects already revealed the quest for such a continuity between the different sections of the house. The renovation of his own home in Wunda Road was a set exercise on the theme, aimed at making the long, highly compartmentalized, existing bungalow easier to live in. In his first new house, for his brother in 1969, he re-affirmed this linear progression from the most public to the most private, starting from the street and running under a narrow flat roof that projects as a portico. The long pavilion eventually became the basic unit of his architecture: sometimes isolated in the country (Ball, Magney at Bingi, and Marika houses), or set on a more urban parcel, whose the division into long narrow plots allows the perpetuation of the form (Muston house). When Murcutt needs to distinguish between living and sleeping areas, or meet the requirements of a large-scale program, his elongated forms are placed in parallel groups of two or three buildings that open on to each other transversally.

The appendages of a building's exterior – a walkway (Ball and Fredericks houses) or a short stair ('Miesian' houses, Kempsey, Marika), that mark the beginning of the journey – reinforce the impression of the finished building's apparent detachment from its site. The walkway generally follows a route that crosses the house from end to end (Magney house at Bingi) or connects different pavilions grafted on to its overall trajectory (Munro and Meagher houses). In the Aboriginal Alcoholic Rehabilitation Centre and the Simpson-Lee house, the layout is entirely structured by the walkways that link and cross between several pavilions.

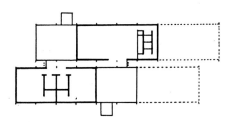

In giving shape to a longitudinal plan that is narrative and dynamic, Murcutt is able to 'track' within the site, like a roving camera. The passage through the interior becomes an unfettered progression, and each moment in the journey through the landscape's vast continuity one of many possible experiences of place.

This journey is always punctuated by an intermediate area between outside and inside, the form and location of which varies from one building to another. Because it is inscribed in the logic and continuity of the plan, it is never an extraneous feature. At the far end of a building, this space is the last stage in the sequence of living areas: a porch open on three sides to the horizon; a terrace or outside platform attached to the house by a light and removable screen. Inserted into this progression of internal spaces, it seems hollowed out, an interruption in the façade, sheltered by the communal roof (Magney house at Bingi) or a covered 'throughway' (museum at Broken Hill). In town houses Murcutt's strategic response to the imperatives of the context is the use of an internal courtyard, patio or atrium. Thus the building has enough nature to achieve the transition of scale between the landscape and interior while jealously guarding domestic privacy. Courtyards are treated as rooms left open to the sky, paved (Done house) or planted (Douglas Murcutt house); atriums act as focal points of living rooms (Ockens house). In every case Murcutt reinterprets, extends and modifies one of the common features of Australian architecture, the veranda, although it is never employed in its traditional form as a portico set against the main façade.

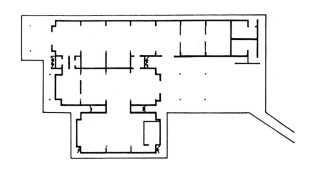

Murcutt clearly delineates 'serving' and 'served' areas, which he organizes in a variety of ways. In his first, Miesian houses, kitchens and bathrooms were grouped within a pivotal central core, independent of the exterior walls, to both define and serve the sleeping and living rooms. In his later work Murcutt designed these functional spaces as interconnected pavilions (Nicholas house, Berowra and Terrey Hills restaurants). He extrapolated on this coupling by joining the wet areas along the longitudinal axis, creating a transversal spine between the 'serving' and 'served' spaces (Littlemore, Magney at Bingi houses). This arrangement has become common:

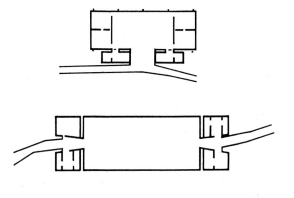

0 2   10m

**Open Living Area of
Constant Height**

Each shelter is adapted to its
surroundings: Ball-Eastaway House,
Magney House, Fredericks House,
Marika-Alderton House, Simpson-
Lee House.

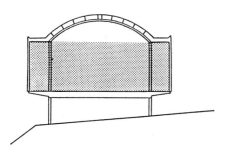

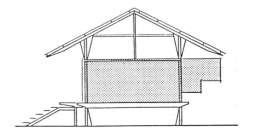

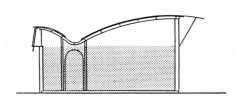

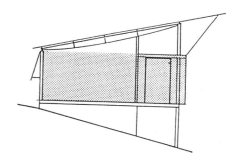

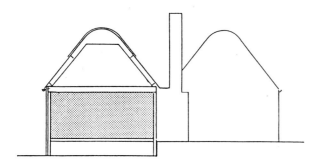

it frees the open plan, allows a rational internal order, and coheres with the plan's linear continuity.

With the serving-served partition set into parallel bands, Murcutt often devises the two long façades, which generally face north and south in opposing manners, a feature that appears in his first house in 1962 and later becomes systematized. On the wind or street side, against which the wet areas are placed, the façade is blind and opaque – clad in timber or metal, or in brick masonry. On the private or protected side, the wall of the living areas is openable or porous, a window wall composed of large glazed sliding doors or louvres. The differentiation of the façades thus reflects both the internal order and the imperatives of orientation in relation to climatic consideration. For Murcutt this in turn corresponds to one of the fundaments of human settlement: to protect oneself on one side while remaining open to the scenery on the other. This notion also recalls Chinese *feng-shui*, or geomancy, whereby the ideal building backs onto a mountain and overlooks a river. Murcutt has discovered similar principles among the Aborigines, who seek to reconcile safety and openness by incorporating both *refuge* (the shelter) and *prospect* (the vista) when they build their bark shelters or move into caves during the rainy season.

Finally, Murcutt brings together all the functions within a common envelope, readable as such from both inside and outside; its long, continuous profile is obtained from a typical cross section as if by extrusion. The fluid plan of the Farnsworth house and the open volume of the woolshed are here again his inspiration. Each returns to the essential theme of minimal shelter and the one-room dwelling. In *Walden, or Life in the Woods* Thoreau described his dream house as having only one vast room, a substantial primitive hall that would support a sort of lower heaven over one's head.[39] Murcutt designs his buildings as a reciprocal double movement: the unification of interior space and the differentiation of the outer envelope's two elements.

Erecting the frame and roof is for Murcutt the fundamental act of construction, one that gives material form to shelter in close relationship with the site and climate. The houses, usually of constant height, have open-plan interiors within walls that act as permeable and fluctuating boundaries. Whether the roof is convex, pitched or single-pitched, the gap between its particular shape and the simple parallelepiped of the living box is left open, affording a global view of the interior while expressing the functional and symbolic roles of enclosed areas (shelter) and covered spaces (dwellings), respectively. Murcutt thus unites in a single building type the archetype of protective shelter with the modernist ideal of a 'free' plan and elevation.

Such a systematic approach, however, has its drawbacks. In most of his pavilions, the aligned rooms have the same ceiling height no matter what their size; the volumes of small rooms, determined by those of the large ones, are sometimes awkward. Façades with long and fairly inaccessible clerestory glazing are difficult to screen; daylight penetrating the house's interior along the sun's trajectory can at times become oppressive. But this unity/duality of the outer envelope, which has evolved over the past six or seven years towards more expansive roofs, more expressionist frames and an increasingly subtle dissolution of boundaries, gives Murcutt's buildings great plastic force.

On the face of it the Magney house at Bingi is an unlikely example of the interaction of the 'objective' forces involved in the articulation of the outer envelope, but it in fact provides a good demonstration. Supported by a metal structure, the house's asymmetric play of curved surfaces shelters a dwelling area 2.1 metres high, formed by metal cladding. The gap between the wing and the box is glazed on the four façades and above the partitions from one end of the building to the other. The roof's form is a function of the different ceiling heights of the three parallel zones within: 3.4 metres on the north façade to capture the light, direct it to the house's centre through the living rooms and give an extensive view of the sea; 2.9 metres for the service band at the back, so that a high window can frame the sky; and between the two is a central passageway under the gutter soffit. The north-side canopy's overhang is calculated to block off the summer sun's vertical rays without obstructing the view. The house presents its lower side to the prevailing cold winds. The roof's two converging slopes are steep enough to ensure efficient water drainage without giving unneces-

Glenn Murcutt
Landscape Interpretation Centre,
National Park of Kakadu
1992. Preliminary sketch (plan), under a
protective wing (section)

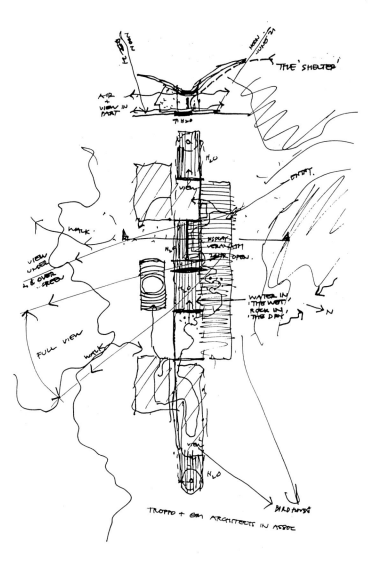

sary purchase to the wind. Lastly, the curves are suggested by the corrugated iron, by nature easier to bend than fold or assemble. Thus, to arrive at the lyrical forms of the Bingi house Murcutt initially followed a quasi-mathematical model guided by the search for an equilibrium between the constraints of plan and site.

AIR, WATER AND LIGHT

One of the most individual aspects of Murcutt's architecture is his use of natural elements for technical, architectural and aesthetic ends. Air, water and light are essential and universal but vary in character from place to place. He integrates their qualities and perenniality into his architecture to inscribe their cyclical characteristics on it, to make them palpable and comprehensible.

Atmospheric phenomena fascinate Murcutt. Sailing, constructing model aeroplanes and boats, aeronautics, and indeed anything pertaining to the 'mathematics of flight' – to cite one of Murcutt's favourite childhood books – are all catalysts in his quest for an architecture of appropriate forms. He continually learns from the effects of perturbation produced by penetration of the air, its efficient utilization by appropriate forms, the loss of weight, the permanent adjustment to unforeseen and changing conditions for optimal functioning.

Murcutt applies this knowledge to architecture. He rejects the techniques of artificial, energy-consuming temperature control, such as air-conditioning. He prefers to create conditions suited to elementary aerodynamics. Organizing a building's circulation by means of convection and natural pressure, Murcutt positions the building to catch the prevailing breezes through flaps or louvres, so that the cross-ventilation cools and airs the interior. As so often, he aims for the practical and the poetric effects all at once. By respecting the path of the wind, he minimizes the building's impact on the site, and with the air's movement the occupants are made aware of its presence.

Rudimentary or sophisticated, ventilation systems are an integral part of Murcutt's buildings. The façade of the Berowra Inn, for ex-

Hassan Fathy
Diagram of a traditional *malqaf* in the
old houses of Cairo

Windsail in a Mining Settlement
Gulgong, New South Wales, c. 1860(?)
*Mitchell Library, State Library of New
South Wales*

ample, is a long, continuous shutter of pivoting glass slats. In a project for the Landscape Interpretation Centre of Kakadu National Park, located in a tropical climate, he designed a great winged roof permeable to the air and set venturi tubes at regular intervals to accelerate the internal circulation – a mechanical and aesthetic technique reminiscent of the ventilators in the Kempsey museum.

In his great mining museum in Broken Hill, Murcutt reinterpreted the traditional Middle Eastern wind trap, or *malqaf*, on the basis of a study by Egyptian architect Hassan Fathy that describes and classifies the sophisticated ancient technique used in certain Cairo residences, where the latitude and climate are comparable to that of Broken Hill. A series of openings in the façade capture the breeze; incoming air is directed towards the ground by wide ducts and cooled by fountains. As the air warms it rises and exits through points at the top of the central space. By convection, this negative pressure encourages the flow of air into the mouth of the *malqaf* and maintains the cycle of natural ventilation. Murcutt later discovered that a similar technique – using a sail to direct the air, and a bucket of water to cool it – was employed in the pits by Australian miners at the end of last century. To transmit the perfumes of the desert into the heart of the building he also places crushed plants in the *malqafs*.

The presence of water – visible or invisible – is often employed as a means to link the building closely to the site's telluric properties. In the Kempsey farm, the pavilions' orientation and the siting of two verandas at opposite ends were determined by a river and a pond located at either end of the property. In the Broken Hill Mining Museum, where the desert terrain's ground water lies close to the surface, water flows into the building's interior at the same level to supply the *malqaf* system. A pool enclosed by a garden acts as a metaphor of an oasis; the water's surface reflects light on to the underside of the roof in summer and illuminates by refraction the open first floor. In the Landscape Interpretation Centre project at Kakadu, planted ponds mirror seasonal change – rain and drought – a notion that adheres to the building's purpose.

Murcutt also seeks to make the circulation of water perceptible and comprehensible in the architecture: mechanisms for collecting,

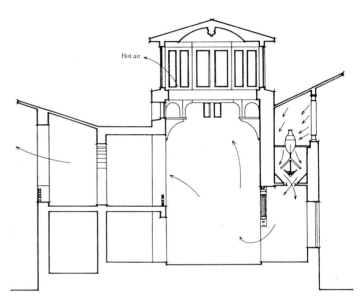

Hot air

storing and draining water are all revealed. The cylindrical corrugated-iron water tanks in the Nicholas and Meagher houses, typical of farms in the outback, are aligned along the façade. In the Done house, the sculptural stainless-steel columnar drainpipes are bracketed together in the middle of the main façade. In the Magney house at Bingi they combine with the horizontal projection of the gutters on either side of the roof to form porticos over the entrances. The roof of the Littlemore house is articulated in progressively steep sections that accelerate the water run-off, which also gives the house its angular profile.

In town houses Murcutt often makes water a physical and symbolic feature. In the Magney house at Paddington, a fountain spills into a long pond that splashes against a window, flashing light into the interior. This edgeless pool is truncated at the far end by an indentation in the garden wall, suggesting the water's mysterious disappearance into infinity. Bubbling spring or mirror inviting contemplation, water is used as a vital element – static or dynamic – with a deferential nod to the 'metaphysical imperative' of Barragán's gardens.[40]

Murcutt regards light as a material of modern architecture, and he makes use of its particular quality in the Australian landscape. The interiors of his buildings are fluid and luminous: contained and homogenous – thanks to the use of uniform colours and materials, white paint and wood cladding, light flows and unifies space. In modifying existing houses Murcutt's first task is to break down partitions to allow the circulation of light entering from limited sources. He also employs traditional methods popular with modern architects, such as using white surfaces to create reflective light and thereby avoid the contrasts of direct sunshine he had observed in Mediterranean villages and some of Aalto's buildings. In the Nicholas house, for example, the north light enters through a band of skylights and bounces off a concave ceiling to illuminate the interior.

Above all Murcutt celebrates the local light's particular character, which he observes in the natural phenomena and landscape. The sunshine is so intense in Australia that leaves assume a vertical position to reduce the angle of incidence on their exposed surfaces

and to limit daytime evaporation. This reaction explains the trees' sparse, transparent look, a characteristic already observed in 1835 by the English landscape artist John Glover, who was amazed that Australian trees do not significantly obstruct long-distance views.[41] In northern Europe, where the climate is more temperate and the light more muted, leaves more readily turn their faces to the sun; vegetation is often close together in opaque masses. In contrast, the intensity of light in most parts of Australia visually separates the elements of the landscape. Murcutt was convinced of this by a number of pictures by the contemporary Australian artist Fred Williams, who portrays expanses of desert scattered with disconnected objects in an apparently random order.

The landscape in the Australian light is thus characterized by its lightness, legibility and discontinuity. Murcutt yields to the sun's effect on the landscape, which is clearly expressed in the individual elements of his architecture. Inside, light is domesticated, subdued; outside, the free and piercing light beats down on the building and reveals its structure. Murcutt's handling of the roof on either side of the house's exterior limits systematically gives form to this contrast. Inside he inserts a smooth or slightly rippled false ceiling, outside he exposes the frame's angular sections and the corrugated iron's rough texture, a transformation revealed through clerestories in the gable ends. He emphasizes assembled sections and meeting points of planes or materials to intercept the shadows that then reinforce their effect. By clearly differentiating the three elements of the Magney house's large veranda – the metal frame, the two chamfered brick walls and the metal roof supported by a slender frame – the role of each plane is determined and its fluctuation is controlled. In the Ball house's gable a transverse section projecting from the façade reveals the skeleton's structure and the skin's composition.

In celebrating the landscape's regional character Murcutt also validates his ideal of 'the truth of structure'. He returns to the classical taste for creating relief on a façade by the use of features that cast shadows: the corner braces of his metal porticos, or the fold in an awning. He detaches the downpipes from the façade by setting them against a curved metal sheet that captures and distorts their

Kempsey Museum
Making a feature of a downpipe
Photo: Max Dupain

shadows. The dull grey of the galvanized sheet metal as its zinc flakes oxidize and lose their silver sheen brings the meticulously placed downpipes into high relief. From his first metal-clad buildings Murcutt has explored the play of faded-metal tones against the vegetation.[42] The Kempsey museum's pavilions, for instance, combine an entire palette of glass and metal textures. The graphic designs – the grooves of corrugated iron, the squared motif of wooden trellises, translucent glass brickwork – interact with the shifting shadows cast by indentations in the wall, by overhanging awnings or glass roofs, or by the trembling leaves of the huge eucalyptuses. The effect – ever-changing according to season, the hour of the day, sun and wind – enhances both architecture and landscape, and imparts an awareness of time.

AN ECOLOGICAL FUNCTIONALISM

In a recent lecture the Finnish architect Juhani Pallasmaa stated: 'Today . . . I cannot imagine any other desirable view of the future than an ecologically adapted form of life where architecture returns to early Functionalist ideals derived from biology. Architecture will again take root in its cultural and regional soil. This architecture could be called Ecological Functionalism . . . this view implies a paradoxical task for architecture. It must become more primitive and more refined at the same time: more primitive in terms of meeting the most fundamental human needs with an economy of expression and mediating man's relation to the world . . . and more sophisticated in the sense of adapting to the cyclic systems of nature in terms of both matter and energy. Ecological architecture also implies a view of building more as a process than a product. And it suggests a new awareness in terms of recycling and responsibility exceeding the scope of life. It also seems that the architect's role between the polarities of craft and art has to be redefined . . . . After the decades of affluence and abundance, architecture is likely to return to the aesthetics of necessity in which the elements of metaphorical expression and practical craft fuse into each other again; utility and beauty again united.'

This proclamation could be a summary of the principles that have long guided Murcutt's work. It posits a constant questioning of human rules, viewed as imperfect and fallible by comparison with the superior law of nature. The consequence of Murcutt's minimalism, expressed as much in his militant ecological choices as in his Miesian affiliation, is his acerbic criticism of contemporary architecture, particularly in Australia.

In their construction, operation and even their future, Murcutt's buildings are designed to consume as little energy as possible. By refining details, he expressed the role of each element as precisely as he can, minimizing materials to economize on natural resources. His knowledge of materials and mastery of manufacturing and construction processes enable him to draw up a descriptive estimate of the ecological cost of each decision in a project, taking into account even labour, a renewable resource. He converts every planned operation into kilojoules, an arithmetical reflex that can yield sometimes unexpected solutions. The reasoning that leads Murcutt to use aluminium over wood casings provides a good illustration. Timber is a renewable resource but has to be sawn and assembled, adding glue and hardware to the reckoning; it also needs to be maintained, with varnish or paint, which also has a cost. Aluminium, on the other hand, consumes much energy in production but can be fully recycled and needs no maintenance.

Murcutt's sense of economy also considers the energy used in temperature regulation. The very substance of his buildings contain the responses to all sorts of climatic conditions. Producing their own shade, ventilation and cooling, they function without air conditioning and in most cases with no heating other than a supplementary fireplace. In the Ockens house, underfloor heating was provided at the request of the clients, who feared the atrium's glass roof would not provide enough heat in winter; the heating has never been used. Murcutt is a keen advocate of ingenious and rational architectural solutions versus the usual recourse to energy consumption. He also pays scrupulous attention to the source of the materials he uses, the conditions under which they are exploited and their renewable nature.

For Murcutt the 'ideal building' would be functionally autonomous – once the required energy has been used for construction – and so be not unlike a windmill or sundial. To illustrate the fundamental difference between 'primitive' and 'modern' societies, Claude Lévi-Strauss compares the former to mechanical machines – those that could theoretically function indefinitely on the energy supplied at the outset, like clocks – and the latter to thermodynamic machines, which are highly productive but consume a great quantity of energy that they steadily destroy, like steam-powered engines.[44] Amidst growing debate in the United States, Scandinavia and Germany on architecture's contribution to industrial societies' ecological future, it is tempting to pursue this analogy in Murcutt's work: in opposition to Western industrial production and the entropy that characterizes it, Murcutt puts forward his sober machines, to be introduced without apparent disturbance to the immutable order of natural cycles.

But how is this ideal be adapted to a more prosaic reality? Australia is among the most urbanized countries on the planet: two-thirds of its eighteen million inhabitants live in the sprawling suburbs of the five main urban agglomerations. Murcutt often assails Australian cities for being no more than business centres drowned in suburbia, where 'people think they are in the country, with the advantages of the town, without really being in either'. He thunders against historicism and fiercely criticizes commonplace houses for being unadapted to the local climate and materials (the balloon-frame bungalows with brick facing and heavy tiled roofs built in the thousands in new speculative developments). In the Sydney suburbs, where Murcutt has often altered existing houses, this model continues to be favoured by municipal regulations. Often, building approvals for his houses have been given only after his successful defence against protracted court actions that claim his projects are incompatible with statutory 'heritage controls'.

Murcutt avers that humans, a transitory presence, should act as custodians, not owners, of the earth and its resources. He sums up his attitude with a maxim attributed to a group of Aborigines in Western Australia: 'Touch this earth lightly', a proverb expressing the ideal relationship, based on sensitivity and respect, that he wants to re-establish with local landscape. Modifiable and extendable, his pavilions on stilts can be demounted and removed without leaving a trace or causing any irremediable destruction to the environment.

Murcutt seeks an equilibrium between a project's technical and functional requirements and the moral imperatives he assigns to it. Such a discipline ensures that his buildings are at one with his conscience and has so far resulted in a frugal architecture invested with a very controlled, almost puritan aesthetic. He wants to validate the original and eternal links with nature, in harmony with its constraints but in counterpoint with its forms. Returning to the classical ideal that a place should be revealed through its architecture, Murcutt makes his buildings – to paraphrase the words of Le Corbusier in *Journey to the East* – the reason for the landscape.

Murcutt's position is not, however, without its contradictions: Owing to the fate of a society and the will of the architect, Murcutt's beliefs have until now been realized almost exclusively in the private house – pillar of Australian life, progenitor of his hated suburbs, greedy consumer of space and infrastructure, indeed the epitome of fragmentary and selfish land use. In the last twenty years Murcutt has created a series of exemplary buildings, mediators between their owners and an implied cosmic ritual, an architecture of singular beauty that harks back to a Europe ever fascinated by the myth of the wild continent and the last frontier.

Notes

1   Unless otherwise stated, all quotations in this text are from the author's notes during numerous conversations with Murcutt between 1989 and 1993.

2   The critic Kenneth Frampton (USA), the architects Sverre Fehn (Norway), Juhani Pallasmaa, Pentii Kareoja (Finland). The jury was presided over by Gunnel Aldercreutz (Finnish Association of Architects) and included, among others, Aimo Murtomaki, Finnish Minister of Education.

3   *Architecture and Arts*, formerly *Architecture and Arts and the Modern Home*, was founded in Melbourne in July 1952 by the Victorian Architecture Students Society.

4   The 'Californian bungalow' was a style of Australian domestic architecture popular in the Twenties.

5   Gordon Drake, 'Modular house on Pacific coast capitalizes on the area's famous topography, climate and materials', *Architectural Forum*, September 1947.

6   Finland and Australia, moreover, somewhat curiously have numerous points in common: both are individualist democracies recently come to independence, which have long searched for a distinct national identity, and face the thorny issue of a marginalized primitive people – Lapps and Aboriginals; both have an almost desert terrain where the architecture seeks to express a symbiosis with the natural landscape. Murcutt's work has been closely followed in Finland for some time.

7   'This is the first house built by Mies van der Rohe...', *Architectural Forum – The Magazine of Building*, special house number, October 1951, pp. 156-61.

8   Reyner Banham: 'Toward a modestly galvo architecture?', *Design Book Review*, vol. 14, 1988.

9   Esther McCoy, *Case Study Houses, 1945-1962*, Hennessy & Ingalls, Los Angeles, 1977.

10 Bill Lucas quoted by Gary Charles Wolff: 'The Sydney School', thesis for Bachelor of Architecture, University of New South Wales, 1984.

11 Glenn Murcutt, 'Group Housing in the Urban Environment', University of New South Wales, 1961.

12 From a letter to his mother Daphne dated 24 August 1964.

13 With John Smith, Keith Cottier and Bruce Bowden, Australian companions of his London days, also passionate about Finland. Their project ranked in the first twenty.

14 For a detailed report on Sydney Ancher's formative years and an exhaustive account of his projects and realizations, see Connie Boesen, 'Sydney Ancher', Sydney University, 1979.

15 The careers of Ancher and Murcutt show uncanny parallels: the same determining influence of Mies; almost exclusively domestic works that seek, each in its own way, to marry modern ideals to particular local conditions; the same struggle with the authorities to impose an architecture judged too audacious - refusal of planning permission, protracted legal cases.

16 The competition for the Main Hall of the University of Newcastle, for which Murcutt was responsible, was published in *L'Architecture d'Aujourd'hui*, no. 142.

17 See Rory Spence, 'Richard Leplastrier. La nature de la maison', *L'Architecture d'Aujourd'hui*, no. 285, February 1993.

18 See Franz Schultze, *Mies van der Rohe, a critical biography*, p. 256. The University of Chicago Press, Chicago and London, 1985.

19 An expression of Kenneth Frampton's.

20 At this point Murcutt knew the Farnsworth house only from publications.

21 Murcutt saw the outside of the Maison de Verre in 1964 on one of his visits to Paris. He thus knew of its existence but not its 'contents'.

22 Mies van der Rohe, 'Aphorisms on architecture and form', 1923.

23 'Glenn Murcutt', *Dictionary of Contemporary Architects*, McMillan Press, London, 1980.

24 Richard Rogers, 'Parigi 1930', *Domus* 443, October 1966.

25 As examples of his sources, Murcutt cites the popularizing lectures of the Australian anthropologist Jennifer Isaacs, and the journalist Penny Tweedie's *This Is My Country: a View of Arnhem Land* (Collins, Sydney, 1985).

26 Glenn Murcutt: transcript of a lecture entitled 'Appropriateness in the modern Australian dwelling', Peter Freeman and Judy Vulker, RAIA Education Division, 1992.

27 See essay by Peter Myers, 'Corrugated Galvanised Iron: The Profile of a National Culture', *Transition*, vol.2, Melbourne, June 1981.

28 See *Australian Woolsheds*, text and photos by Harry Sowden, Cassell Australia, Sydney, 1972.

29 Reyner Banham, 'Towards a modestly galvo architecture?', op. cit.

30 Philip Johnson, *Mies van der Rohe*, MOMA, New York, 1953; revised third edition, 1978.

31 Glenn Murcutt, preface to Philip Drew, *Leaves of Iron*, The Law Book Company, 1985.

32 See Bernard Smith, *European Vision and the South Pacific*, third edition, Oxford University Press, 1989.

33 Glenn Murcutt, speech on receiving the RAIA Gold Medal for the education of architectural students, Sydney, 1 July 1992.

34 The work and teachings of McHarg, highly influential in the United States, are set out in his treatise *Design with Nature* (Doubleday and Natural History Press, New York, 1969). Since 1990 Murcutt has been adjunct professor at the School of Landscape Architecture, Graduate School of Fine Arts, University of Pennsylvania, on the invitation of Professor Anne Whiston Spirn, one of McHarg's disciples.

35 Glenn Murcutt, speech on receiving the RAIA Gold Medal, 1 July 1992.

36 'Glenn Murcutt': *Dictionary of Contemporary Architects*, op.cit.

37 Glenn Murcutt, preface to *Leaves of Iron*, ibid.; speech on receiving RAIA Gold Medal, 1 July 1992.

38 See the careful study of the preliminary drawings for the museum in Broken Hill: Haig Beck and Jackie Cooper, UME, box 1, portfolio 1, Melbourne, 1992.

39 Henry David Thoreau, *Walden, or Life in the Woods*, chapter 13. This precise passage was earlier cited by René Herbst in relation to...Chareau ('Pierre Chareau', *Les Arts Ménagers*, Paris, 1954). In this text, Herbst reported that a New York friend of Chareau's, while doubting that the latter had read Thoreau, compared his one-room house in East Hampton to the dream house described in Walden.

40 The expression comes from Emilio Ambasz, *The Architecture of Luis Barragán*, The Museum of Modern Art, New York, 1976.

41 Reported by Bernard Smith, op. cit.

42 Since the Seventies, traditional corrugated iron has gradually been replaced by zincalume - sheet iron coated in zinc and aluminium alloy, whiter and shinier in appearance than the traditional galvanization in pure zinc.

43 Juhani Pallasmaa, 'From metaphorical to ecological functionalism', text of a lecture given in 1991 at the 5th Aalvar Aalto symposium in Jyvaskyla, published in Architectural Review, June 1993, pp. 74-9.

44 From Georges Charbonnier, *Entretiens avec Claude Lévi-Strauss*, René Julliard et Plon, Paris, 1961.

Magney House
Paddington, Sydney, 1987–90

Selected Buildings and Projects

Glenn Murcutt House
Mosman, Sydney
1968–69

After setting up his one-man studio, Murcutt's first project was the renovation of his own home, a bungalow on a narrow block in a comfortable suburb on Sydney's North Shore.

He entirely reconstructed the back of the house, removing the partitions from what had been a series of rooms arranged *en enfilade* giving on to a veranda. While retaining the existing building's walls and floor levels, he reorganized the space into a logical and fluid progression from dining to sitting room, on to an outside platform and the garden beyond. Each stage is demarcated by a step and a change in flooring: cork, timber and cement paving. Murcutt removed all side windows except those facing north. The dining area is skylit and the garden façade is entirely glazed. Murcutt chose Le Corbusier and Bauhaus furniture (Marcel Breuer and Mart Stam), while lighting and other fittings reflect the influence of Arne Jacobsen and Scandinavian design.

Murcutt has clearly adapted the exterior image of Farnsworth House to the purposes and scale of this modest project: his allusions to Mies van der Rohe's work are obvious in the two suspended levels linked by a stair on the garden side of the house, the small off-centre posts supporting the outside platform, the horizontality of the glazed façade, the exclusive use of white to unify the renovation, and in the organization of the living areas as a sequence opening to the outside, a theme which recurs in later projects.

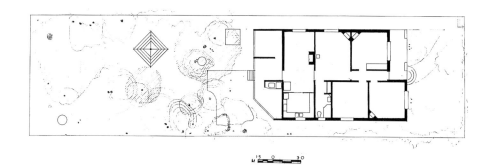

Views of the veranda and living-room

Douglas Murcutt House
Belrose, Sydney
1969–72

On an irregular block in a residential subdivision in the vast suburbs of Sydney, Murutt designed a house for his brother and brother's wife (both music teachers) and their two children. Murcutt adopted a layout that enclosed the house and garden behind a high brick wall to ensure privacy.

The plan was conceived in two perpendicular axes. From the road, a longitudinal passage – given form by a portico and corridor on either side of the main glazed façade – leads from the more public to the most private areas. The garage and music room are left outside the wall; followed in the progression by the sitting room and the family room (a traditional Australian domestic space). From the garden Murcutt transversally organized a gradual transition from outside to inside, with the living areas to the north of the bedrooms. At the intersection of the two axes, the wet rooms are grouped in a compact block, inspired by that of Farnsworth House.

Painted white, the house has a structure with external off-centre columns. The north façade is composed of large sliding-glass doors set in aluminium frames. On the south, the bedrooms, which face a small courtyard, receive refracted sunlight from the white-painted wall opposite. Sliding doors are used throughout, except for the bathrooms, Flooring inside is laid in cork tiles, outside in concrete. As in his own house in Mosman, Murcutt designed the built-in furniture in white melamine and selected Marcel Breuer chairs and Poulsen ceiling lights.

The project reflects Murcutt's continuing exploration of the Miesian vocabulary, adapting it to the conditions of suburban family life as the Californian architects had done before him. In giving the house an enclosed garden planted only with Australian species, he also introduced one of the prevailing ideas of his work: that domestic architecture should preserve its immediate and private relationship with an idealized nature.

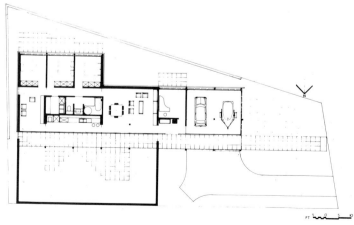

A glass wall divides the kitchen area
from the portico which leads on to
the garden

Laurie Short House
Terrey Hills, Sydney
1972–73

The house is situated on a high, wild site on the edge of Ku-Ring-Gai Chase National Park, on Sydney's northern boundary. The exceptional twelve-kilometre view and the absence of nearby buildings allowed Murcutt to design a transparent building. At the request of the client, the house sits directly on the ground; an abandoned project shows that Murcutt originally envisaged it on stilts.

At the centre of the simple rectangular plan, day rooms and night rooms are distributed on either side of the wet rooms. Entrance to the house is through a narrow gap between the dining room's semicircular wall and the study. The space then opens out, to the north-east, where the inter-communicating kitchen, living room and veranda all open out to the landscape. Metal Venetian blinds and a slatted sun-deflector on the roof reduce the heat and control light levels. Terracotta tiles are laid inside, brick paving outside. The white walls and ceilings contrast with the exposed metal frame, realized in a Miesian manner as corner I-beams. The façades are glazed or clad in matt-black tiling. The colour was inspired by Murcutt's first impression of the site, which he visited after a forest fire had reduced it to a field of charred tree trunks and ash. The house is fitted with an external system of roof sprinklers for fire protection.

The layout and choice of materials indicate that Murcutt envisioned the house as a purely artificial object contrasting with the landscape. He confirmed here his Miesian direction as a reaction to the Wrightian tendency of the Sydney School. In incorporating a veranda and natural climatic-regulation systems for the first time, he also expressed his notion of the relationship between architecture and nature that anticipates the Marie Short house in Kempsey.

Plan and view of the front of the house
with veranda

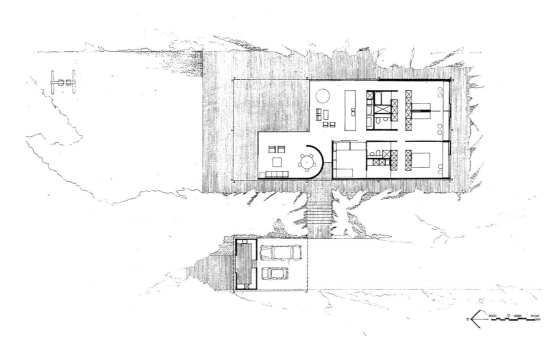

View of the internal space of the living
room, with metallic Venetian blinds and
horizontal brise-soleil

Marie Short House
Kempsey, New South Wales
1974–75 and 1980 (extension)

Kempsey is a small town in dairy-farming country near the coast, some five hundred kilometres north of Sydney. The site, part of a vast agricultural property of woods and grasslands, has a small dam to the east and a river to the west. In summer, cool breezes come from the north-east, and in winter, cold winds blow from the west. The Kempsey house was commissioned in 1975 by Marie Short, who had bought the property some years before and wanted to extend the existing farm.

Because of its distance from Sydney, Murcutt was only able to make site visits every three weeks. He was thus restricted to using simple details and techniques familiar to local firms that were accustomed to building farms and cottages. Materials needed to be locally available and the components taken from a catalogue – standard glazing, corrugated iron and louvres. Furthermore, the client had already collected a variety of Australian and American woods in anticipation of the building work. The estimated construction cost of 120 square metres was then about $30,000A.

The house was designed for three people, including a permanent resident. Murcutt sited it on the edge of a broad grassland area, at the top of a slight slope leading down to the farm. The house is made up of two symmetrical pavilions that are staggered in relation to each other and coupled longitudinally on either side of a wide gutter. The communal living areas are grouped in the north wing, along the length of the winding river, facing the sun. Murcutt combined the kitchen with the living room, as he had in the Laurie Short House. The south wing contains two bedrooms. Both wings

are equipped with a sanitary block, and each has a veranda at one end that extends the space while transversally serving the adjoining wing as a porch.

The house is constructed as a series of Oregon pine post-and-beam frames set at three-metre intervals. Fitted into this structure are modules of metal-and-glass louvres (four per three-metre frame), insect screens and aluminium Venetian blinds. The floor is raised 0.8 metres above the ground on stilts. The gables are faced in cedar boards, with gaps at the top to ventilate the underside of the roof. The two pavilions are attached by metal tie-rods that support the central gutter, and they give into each other through two large pivoting doors. The roof is made of corrugated

iron, bent according to building techniques used for traditional watertanks. The interior fittings are of Australian hardwood: walls and ceiling are faced with horizontal strips of hoop pine and the floor is laid with brush box. The entire wooden interior has a Scandinavian atmosphere that is accentuated by Aalto lights and furniture. Designed to be extendable and demountable, the house has a minimal foundation, a modular frame (held together by nuts and bolts), and employs repetitive elements.

Murcutt bought the house in 1980 and was able to enlarge and reorganize it for the needs of his own family. He added two bays to each pavilion, demounting the gables and verandas and

replacing them at the new ends. Everything was reused. The new configuration made each wing more independent, the original division of day-night becoming parents-children.

In this house Murcutt has achieved a harmonious synthesis of his concurrent reflections on modern and traditional architecture. The reference to Mies van der Rohe is invigorated by his discovery of traditional construction techniques and climatic regulation used in Australian farm buildings, and in so doing he achieves clarity, legibility and precise adaptation to the site. The Kempsey house is, if not a manifesto, a seminal work that explains and significantly shapes his later development.

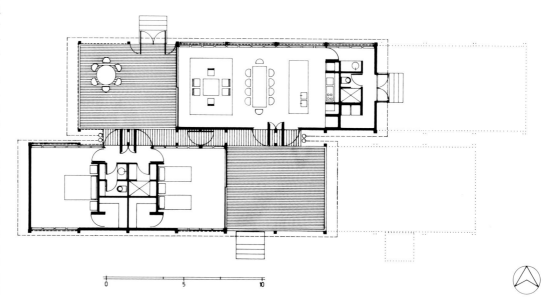

0   5   10

Plan of the enlarged building and an end
view of the two blocks

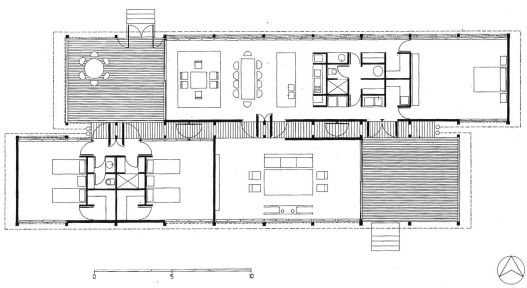

0   5   10

Detail of a section and a view showing
the corrugated-iron roof and the metallic Venetian blinds

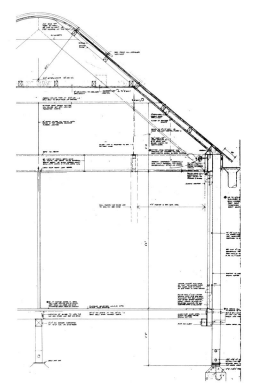

Ockens House
Cromer, Sydney
1977–78

This house is located in the hills of a northern Sydney suburb, above the Narrabeen lakes not far from the coast. The elongated site (twenty by fifty metres) is oriented north-south. Planning regulations obliged Murcutt to align the façade with the adjoining houses and thus place the building at the top of the slope, squeezed on to the end of the plot.

To make the most of the view the living rooms were placed as high as possible. From the road below, the house looks like two blind symmetrical brick boxes flanking a protrusion that opens out to the north. The black steel frame, which supports a loggia extending out over the ground floor, balances the house's horizontality and contrasts with the side walls' massive verticality. The entrance contains a sculptural metal staircase leading to the upper floor.

To preserve domestic privacy Murcutt planned a radically introverted layout. Contained within a totally opaque envelope, the cruciform plan distributes all the house's spaces on three sides of an atrium. The fourth side provides a distant view of the lakes through large sliding doors opening on to the loggia. Covered by wide-slatted Venetian blinds, edged with louvres, the atrium is a sun-trap that provides natural light and interior ventilation. Its glazed roof is supported by round metal columns, some of which function as downpipes. It is also covered by a layer of pivoting brise-soleil. The atrium's floor, fractionally lower than the adjoining rooms, is laid with terracotta tiles and planted with tropical vegetation.

The Ockens house provides an example of the suburban residences that Murcutt designed after the Kempsey farmhouse. In these projects he temporarily abandoned the vernacular form while retaining its lessons on light and climate. The Ockens house's organization and vocabulary are reminiscent of certain Californian or Finnish houses of the 1960s, such as Craig Ellwood's Daphne residence in Los Angeles or Toivo Korkonen's house near Helsinki.

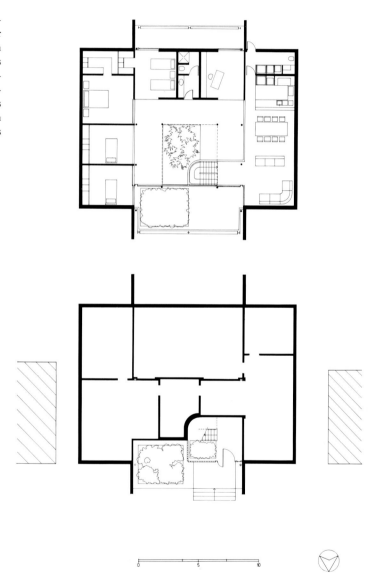

View of the front of the house, the loggia bordered by two solid brick walls, and a section through the slope of the site

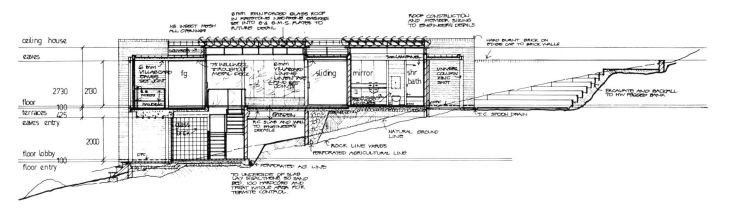

Two views of the cloistered entrance hall and a study of the front of the house facing the slope

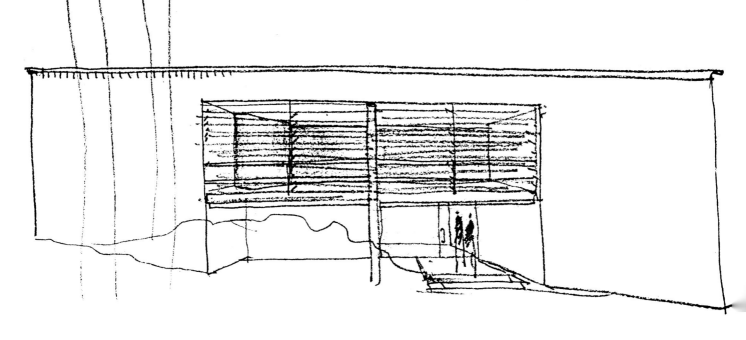

View of the study with the and a sketch
of the front of the house incorporating
the loggia

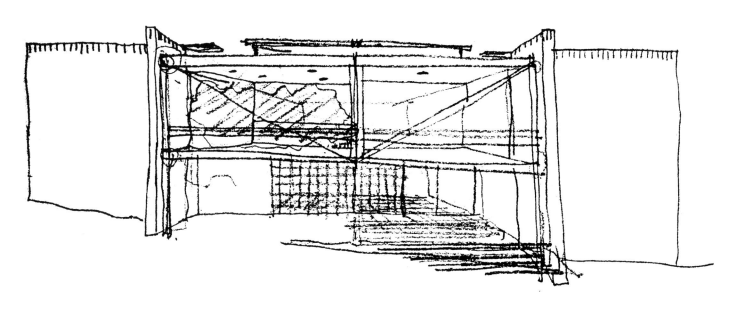

Nicholas House
Mount Irvine, New South Wales
1977–80

This residence is one of two 'country houses' built by Murcutt for two families of lawyers who use them as weekend homes. It is situated in an agricultural region of the Blue Mountains, some 120 kilometres north-west of Sydney, on a slight slope of an open plateau, with wide-ranging views.

The house consists of two pavilions that vary in dimension, form and function. Raised slightly above the ground, they are linked longitudinally by a large 'box-gutter'. Beneath a large sloping roof, the main pavilion contains a veranda, living-dining room and bedrooms on two levels, arranged in a linear progression from the east entrance. With its stunning view, the north façade is glazed with louvres, backed by external cedar Venetian blinds, and closed as it abuts the bedrooms. The rear pavilion houses the kitchen and bathrooms, supplied by rain-water tanks and storage areas. The roof is curved on one side to deflect prevailing winds, which run along the slope. The house's south side is clad entirely in corrugated iron, laid horizontally from floor to roof level, without a single opening. The division into two pavilions – 'serving' and 'served', clearly legible on the outside – is blurred inside by the absence of a partition between the kitchen and living room, which unifies the central space and creates its wider transverse area. Capturing the reflected north light, the ceiling's soffit illuminates the kitchen.

Sydney's proximity and the site's relative isolation lead the choice of materials towards standard parts, with the exception of local pine for interior panelling. The dimensions of the frame and woodwork and the required construction techniques were planned to enable the building of the entire house *in situ* by one craftsman.

The Nicholas house marks the start of Murcutt's use of corrugated iron as cladding. Murcutt organizes the living areas and bathrooms in parallel bands for the first time, which led him to the opposite treatment of the long elevations. The house is remarkable for the contrast between the rustic character of the front and the steel curves at the back.

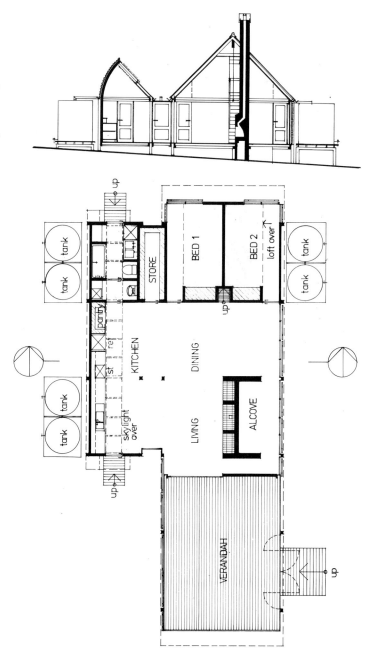

Views from the east and west

Sketch of the transverse section including notes on the effects of wind and sunlight and a view of the interior

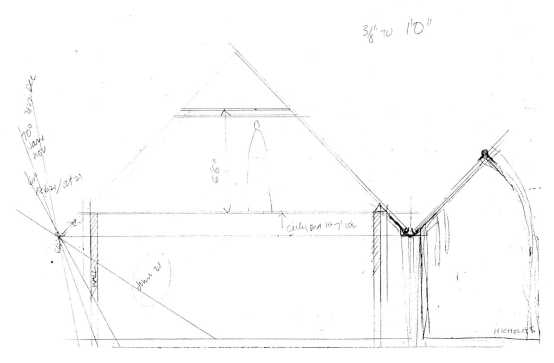

Berowra Waters Inn
Sydney
1977–78 and 1982–83

An hour north of central Sydney, the Berowra River widens and flows through a wild and rugged gorge. On its west bank, in an old tea-house dating back to the twenties, two well-known Sydney chefs, Tony and Gay Bilson, wanted to create a simple and elegant setting that would attract customers as much for the place as for the gastronomic experience.

The present structure was built in two phases. In the first Murcutt restructured the old building, which was on the point of collapse, to provide a dining room with seating for fifty-five, a kitchen, essential storage space, staff quarters. All the work was executed by two builders from Melbourne.

In the second phase, Murcutt dug out the hill behind the building to make room for a pavilion to house the facilities. He also added a studio for the owners at the restaurant's western end. A third phase is planned to extend the diagonally positioned stairs into a promenade that climbs up the riverbank.

The restaurant has no access by land – diners are taken by boat to a pontoon below the entrance. Murcutt retained the existing floor levels of the original building and placed the servant areas at the rear of the building, against the slope. The ground-level wall was rebuilt with large pieces of sandstone rubble; a cavity within it contains the stairs up to the dining room, which overlooks the water. On the first floor a large glazed façade has replaced the old veranda. Behind a new independent steel frame is a continuous membrane of louvres, which takes full advantage of the panorama and can be adjusted to suit the climate and to catch the water's shifting reflections of the light.

The dining room is long and narrow, so that every table has a view of the river, and extends on to a terrace at its eastern end. The roof is of pale-blue-painted corrugated iron. The transparence of the dining room's façade is visible from afar, thus functioning also as a kind of signboard. The rustic sandstone wall echoes the rocks of the neighbouring cliffs and contrasts with the crystalline delicacy of the glazed wall.

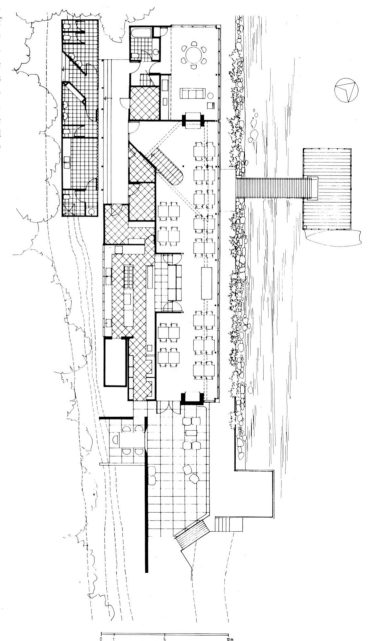

General layout and a view of the entrance to the service block

Views from inside and out over the river
with the large glass window containing
louvres on the first floor.

The dining room, kitchen and internal
staircase

Local History Museum and Tourist Office
Kempsey, New South Wales
1976/1979–82, 1986–88

Situated on the town's southern edge beside the highway linking Sydney and Brisbane, the Kempsey museum lies on a large site shaded by magnificent eucalyptuses. The climate is warm in winter and very hot in summer, tempered by cool north-easterly breezes from the nearby ocean.

The current building was constructed in two phases with a five-year interval. The first phase included the construction of an exhibition hall and storerooms for the local history museum with the potential to extend, as well as a tourist office, small assembly and projection room. Several architectural reconstructions of early pioneer buildings (a cottage, school and windmills) were to be erected around the new building. The budget was small, dependent on funds and grants provided by the New South Wales government and Kempsey Shire council.

For the museum to be on a domestic scale similar to that of the reconstructed historic cottage south of the museum building, Murcutt followed the divisions inherent in the program: three principal elements were arranged into three parallel pavilions, distinct but interrelated. The central pavilion, which contains the entrance, reception and tourist office, gives lateral access to the other two: the north wing's exhibition hall and the south wing's theatre. The simple, repeated construction system defines the outer envelope and delineates areas according to a structural order. The building rests on a simple coloured-concrete base. The building is enclosed by brick walls insulated on the exterior and clad in zincalume. Internally, the walls are punctuated at four-metre intervals with vertical braces that bind the exhibition bays.

The tubular metal frame supports the convex corrugated-iron roof.

At the junction of roof and walls, clerestories screened by Venetian blinds illuminate the exhibition bays. Ventilation is provided by wooden flaps at the top of the walls and by factory-made extractors on the roof. The gable end of each pavilion either incorporates a veranda with red-cedar trellises or is just closed off. The transversal communication from one pavilion to the other is beneath the gutters, which demarcate the interior's wide service bands containing lavatories and storage areas. This first phase, covering some four hundred square metres, was completed for $265,000A.

In 1986 the museum association commissioned Murcutt to do the second phase. He naturally positioned new pavilions as extensions of the previous ones, built with the same structural system and linked by the same principle. The north wing was opened at the gable end and enlarged by four frames; the central pavilion was extended by six frames so that the veranda inserted at the junction with the tourist office would differentiate the functions; a south wing was added to balance the theatre. The museum's three parts (phase 1, phase 2 and the reconstructed cottage) are now linked by a central courtyard focusing on the cottage; trees are planted in a grid and aligned with the buildings' frames.

Murcutt has magnified the banal Australian country building and its ordinary materials in close accord with the site, budget and program – specifically, a collection of popular arts and traditions. In his subsequent projects, he continues this highly personal assemblage of different metal forms and explores their expressiveness.

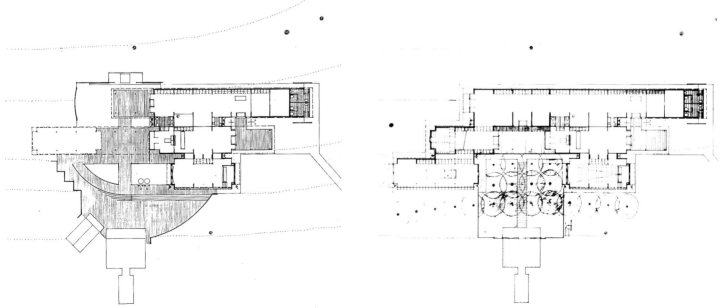

End-view of the north wing used for
exhibitions

Details of the ends and the juxtaposition
of two of the pavilions; interior views of
the theatre and exhibition hall

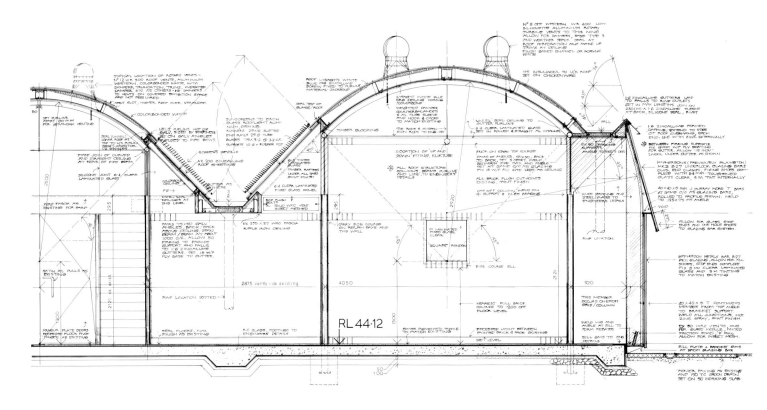

Ball-Eastaway House and Studio
Glenorie, Sydney
1980–83

In a forest of acacias, eucalyptuses and banksias, Murcutt built a house for two artists on a ten-hectare site on the edge of the Marramarra National Park, north-west of Sydney. The residence is situated on top of a series of sandstone ledges, characteristic of the region's terrain, which rises gently to the north-west. The frame, comprising seven tubular-steel portals anchored to the rock, supports the floor – a wooden platform raised above ground level – and a convex metal roof. The space is enclosed lengthwise on both sides by a corrugated-iron–insulation–plasterboard sandwich interrupted by openings corresponding to the interior's organization. Two large flat gutters on the sides create a right-angled junction of roof and walls; a sprinkler system on the roof protects against forest fires.

Living rooms and bedrooms are placed at either end of the house. A wide corridor/exhibition gallery links them longitudinally. Kitchen, bathrooms and storage space are grouped against the blind south façade. The two gables are completely glazed. There are two verandas: a small self-contained deck inserted into the north-west façade framing the landscape, and a large area open on three sides extending out from the living room in the north-east. Murcutt took particular care with the larger veranda's edges, which grow progressively finer as they move from earth to sky. The impression of a precarious but tranquil equilibrium between construction and landscape is accentuated by the delicate wood entrance walkway, the view of the ground beneath the house, and the treatment of the outer walls as suspended planes.

The Ball house, which owes as much to the Marie Short house as to the Kempsey museum, is one of Murcutt's most successful buildings. It epitomizes the lightweight, linear, economical and elegant pavilion, minimal in its environmental impact.

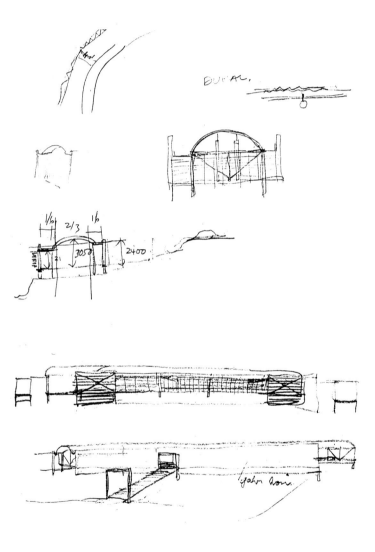

View of the north-west façade and plan

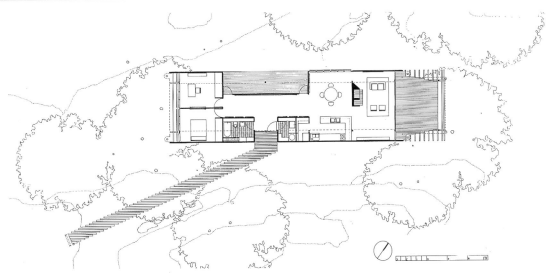

Elevations and a view of the house from
the south-east

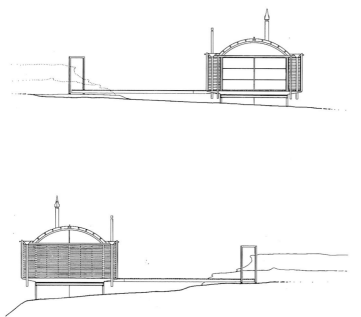

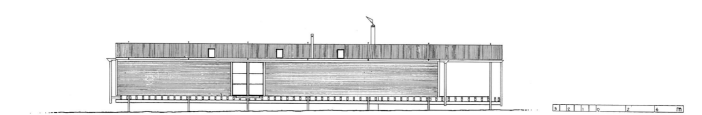

Details of the corrugated-iron wall and
drainpipe; north-west elevation

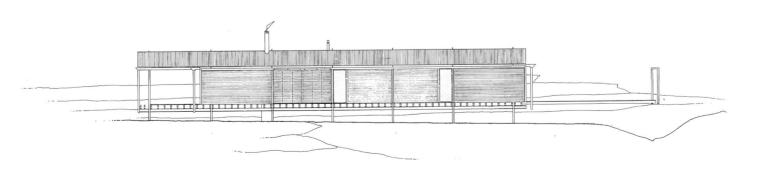

Transverse and longitudinal sections, including a detail through the bathroom, and a view along the gallery corridor

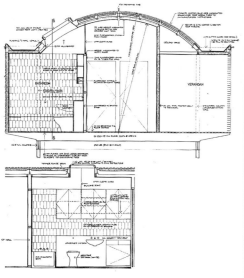

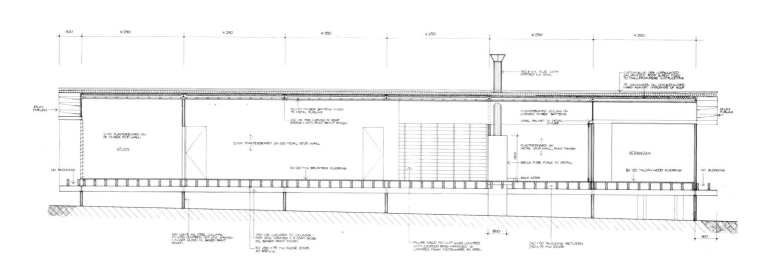

Views of the bedroom end of the house
and the veranda, and two cross sections

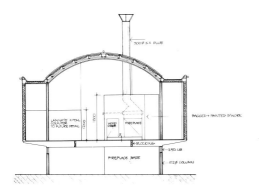

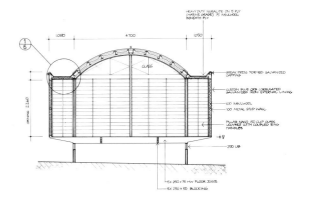

Fredericks House
Jamberoo, New South Wales
1981–82

Fredericks house is located about one hundred kilometres south of Sydney in rich farming country with a cool, rainy climate. Situated on a hillside, it has long sea views to the north. Murcutt made use of an old farm to benefit from the previous occupants' modifications. The house stands on a narrow, levelled ridge that falls away to a wild and spectacular rocky slope on the north and east.

With a total floor area of some two hundred square metres, the new building comprises two adjoining pavilions, similar in outline but different in size. The main pavilion, on stilts, is long and slender: a little over thirty metres long and five metres wide. Murcutt placed the living areas and parents' bedroom at one end and the children's rooms on two levels in the other wing. A connecting veranda between the pavilions is a room in its own right – simultaneously an entrance hall, access to each 'territory' and sitting room, heated by a large fireplace in winter, and a partly open extension to the living room in summer.

Formerly a garage, the other pavilion, resting on the ground, was transformed into a playroom, then an extra bedroom, thus extending the residential accommodation into an L-shape. The north façade is entirely glazed by large sliding-glass doors with insect screens and wood Venetian blinds. The wet rooms are placed along the south façade, which apart from two small high windows for the kitchen and bathroom is completely closed to the cold winds that gust down the valley in winter.

The wooden frame is made of eucalyptus (iron bark), the external cladding of western red cedar, and the internal panelling of pine. In its form, construction system, materials, components and details, Fredericks house adheres to the 'Marie Short model', although the pitch of the roof (high and angled at sixty degrees), has been altered to accommodate a bedroom beneath the eaves.

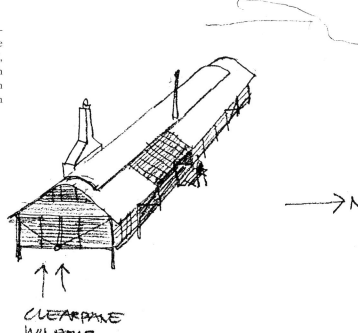

CLEARPANE WINDOWS

$\rightarrow$ N

Aerial view of the building and plan

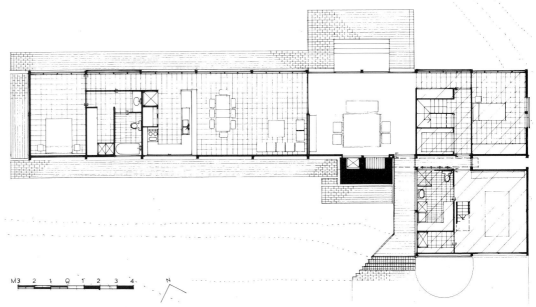

M 3 2 1 0 1 2 3 4   N

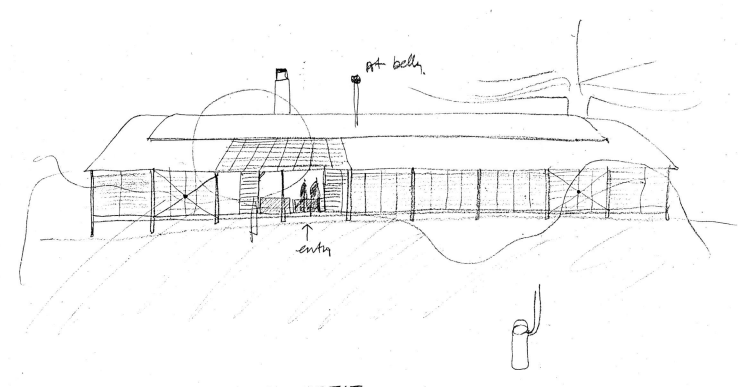

pot belly.

entry

— ON THESE HOUSES I HAVE MOST OF THE
DETAILS ON FILE - BOTH CONSTRUCTION AND
INFILL AS WELL AS VENTILATION — Glenn

— TO DOCUMENT THIS, I WOULD NEED
2 - 3 WEEKS - IT'S WORTHWHILE I FEEL —

G. MURCUTT
OCT 81
FREDERICKS

View from the west (opposite), cross-sectional sketch and view of the interior

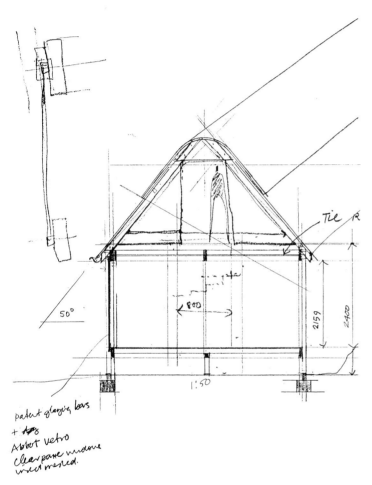

patent glazing bars
+ gg
Abbot Vetro
clearpane windows
uncoatmented.

50°

Tie R

2159

2400

FOD

1:50

Magney House
Bingi Point, New South Wales
1982–84

Magney House was constructed on thirty-three hectares on the Pacific shores near the small town of Moruya, 350 kilometres south of Sydney. To the east lies the Bingi headland, to the north a beach and a lake surrounded by forest – a bare, virtually treeless, seaside setting. Murcutt's clients, who for years had gone to camp there, wanted a lightweight shelter, closer to a tent than a country house, in direct communion with nature. They also wanted a practical, simple and open house that would reflect their informal holiday lifestyle, and an internal organization that would link two independent areas: one for themselves, and the other for children, family and friends.

Weighing the risks of increased exposure against the benefits of the view, Murcutt chose a fairly high position on the slope (when the foundations were dug, evidence of earlier habitation was discovered). He designed a long pavilion facing the lake and sea, with its backs to the distant hills. The living rooms are positioned on the north side and the facilities on the south, in two parallel bands either side of a longitudinal passage, which is open in some places and acts a corridor in others. Under one roof Murcutt brings together two parts corresponding to two families, their respective living rooms mirroring each other across a communal veranda.

The roof, an apparently free form, reflects the climatic consideration of the sun's varying penetration through the seasons, and its outline is adapted to the prevailing winds' force and direction and to the interior ceiling heights. The rear elevation, which faces the cold south winds, is built of brick to a height of 2.1 metres, cul-minating in a sloping glass roof running down its full length. In the gap provided between the bottom of this screen and the top of the opaque wall are a series of narrow, pivoting wooden slats that allow for interior cross-ventilation in the summer. The great north façade, which rises to a height of 3.4 metres, is entirely glazed.

Preliminary sketches indicate that at one point Murcutt envisaged two storeys of bedrooms, as in the Fredericks and Nicholas houses. This solution would have given the house an appropriate proportion to the splendour of the site. In the realized project, which has only one storey, Murcutt retained the idea of a high façade to provide maximum views and to allow as much light as possible into the interior. The large sliding-glass doors, which replaced the louvres that were initially envisaged, are better suited to the climate and permit access from every room. The north façade is fitted with large aluminium Venetian blinds, and the gable is partly glazed to frame the view of the headland.

The house rests on a concrete slab. Beneath it are a small cellar and rainwater tanks fed by two columnar downpipes. The metal frame is composed of porticos, through which the lengthwise passage runs. L-shaped columns form the corners of the glazed box. The purlins of these elements have a sinuous shape created by the assembly of three curved metal tubes. On the south façade, trapezoidal pieces of wood come down to meet the top of the brick wall. The roof is of galvanized corrugated iron.

Inside, Murcutt concealed the roof's frame behind a white curved-plasterboard ceiling. All the dividing brick walls are brick up to a height of 2.1 metres, above which they are glazed to roof level. The fleeting view of the roof's underside, like a wing in motion, emphasizes the transversal movement of space and light.

From afar the house looks like a silver line on the hill, the roof line like a frozen movement against the base's static rectangle. The Bingi house is the lyrical apotheosis of a 'type' invented by Murcutt: the long metal pavilion, in counterpoint to the forms of nature but in harmony with its constraints – the embodiment of the ideals of continuity and unity that he attributes to the orders of nature and architecture.

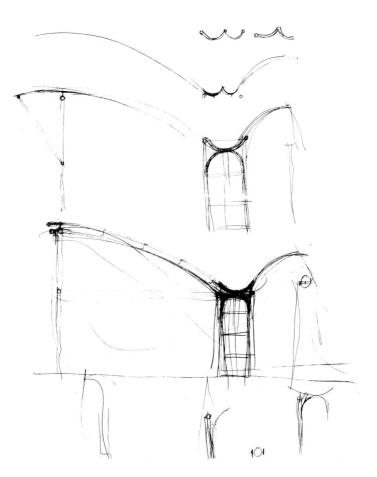

Preliminary section sketches, design of
one end of the house and plan

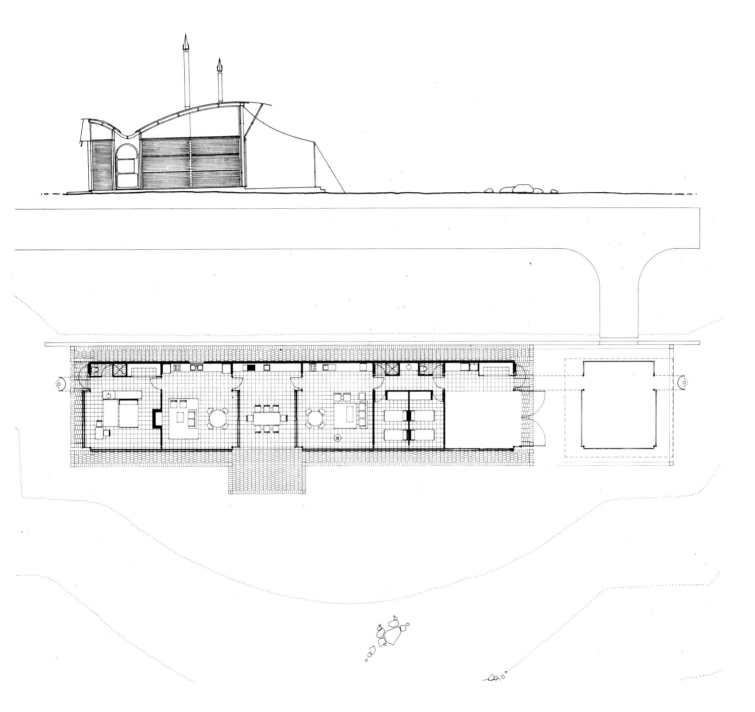

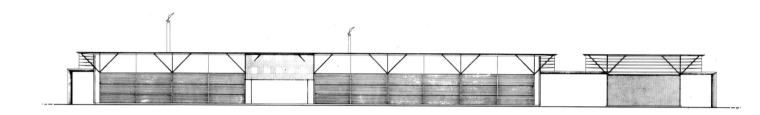

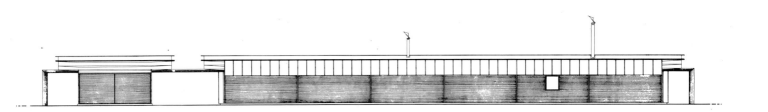

Littlemore House
Woollahra, Sydney
1983–86

Located in a residential urban district of east-central Sydney, the Littlemore house rests on a narrow site (roughly 28 x 5.8 metres) at the end of a row of houses that gives widthwise on to a lane and lengthwise on to a garden square. Instead of conforming to the unfavourable layout suggested by the land division, which would have meant that the small side on the lane was the principal façade, Murcutt rotated the orientation of the house by ninety degrees so that it faces the sun and the square to the north.

The interior layout of the house, his first in such an urban context, is akin to that of projects in the open country, such as the Nicholas and Magney houses. He placed services and passages along the back of the building in a continuous 2.3-metre-wide band, which is set against the blind party wall and skylit. On to this spine he grafted two lightweight metal pavilions separated by a small court-yard. The courtyard's tall proportions are accentuated by its division into vertical modules, imparting an urban ambience to the garden-square façade.

Taking advantage of the site's west-ward slope, Murcutt inserted the garage and entrance in a small ground-floor area facing the street, which allows the level of the living areas to be re-established on the floor above. Inside, the living room, which occupies the building's full width, opens laterally on to a succession of outer rooms. The veranda transforms the kitchen into a summer dining room flanked by a screen of glass bricks that provides privacy from the square. On the second floor, the bed-rooms in each pavilion are distributed so that the usual division of parents and children is maintained. The three children's bedrooms are conceived as small duplexes.

On all the ceilings Murcutt used ripple iron; the floors are laid with parquet in the living rooms, terracotta tiles in the service band, and brick paving in the courtyard and terrace.

The principal façade and plans of the
two levels

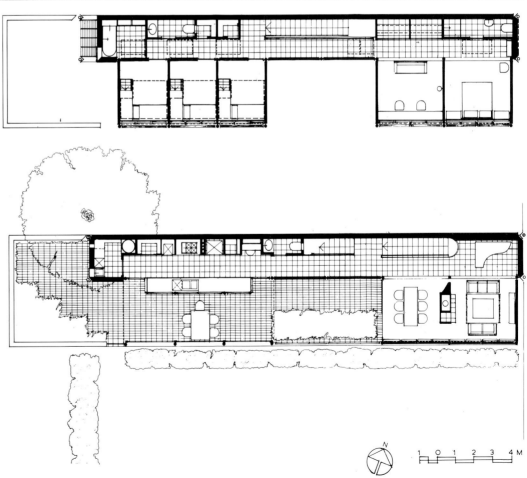

Cross section of the double-height
room and the upper-floor children's
room

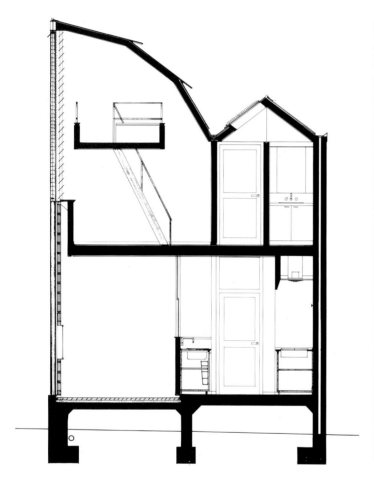

1   0   1   2   3 M

Aboriginal Alcoholic Rehabilitation Centre (Project)
Bennelong's Haven, Kinchela Creek, New South Wales
1983–85

Linked to the anti-alcohol campaign aimed at the Aborigines, this project was entrusted to Murcutt following the centre director's visit to the Kempsey museum. Intended to replace an outdated building, it was originally to have been financed by the local authorities and federal government but they abandoned its realization.

Murcutt's proposed layout based on the topography, climate, his sensitivity to the territory and the assumption that architecture can play a therapeutic role through the conditions it creates and the relationship it encourages between its inhabitants and the environment. The project included community services (medical consultations, activity and assembly areas, restaurant facilities) and patient accommodation.

The proposed buildings, the culmination of long discussions between the architect and all other participants, looks more like a village than a hospital. Patients are dispersed among small, autonomous, communal pavilions, so they don't have to be separated from their family and friends. In determining the siting and type of accommodation, Murcutt examined the Aboriginal family structure to respect the traditional divisions of groups (men-women, young-old men, married-unmarried women).

Located not far from Kempsey, in an area regularly flooded by the McLeay River, the terrain has a shallow relief shaped like a glove – four subsidiary ridges extend eastward from a larger one running north-south. The buildings are positioned in line with the relief, on stilts a half-metre above the maximum floodwater height.

Communal services are grouped along the main promontory in two main buildings on either side of a covered gallery. The residential pavilions are set perpendicularly with the four east-west promontories. Each pavilion is a long house, with a north-facing main façade and clearly differentiated living areas and utility rooms. The complex is linked by a network of narrow wooden walkways, which converge on the service building while remaining at a tangent to the large veranda outside the communal dining room.

Murcutt has sought to combine his own European conception of space and place with that of the Aborigines.

The overall plan suggests the continuity, the 'unfinished' character, of the different routes. The architecture, lightweight and permeable to the elements (reminiscent of the Ball-Eastaway house, which was started at the same time), expresses the transient and reversible nature of the buildings' occupation of the site.

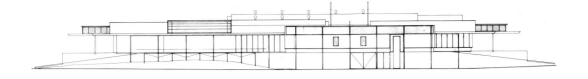

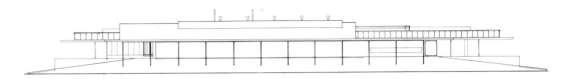

East, west, south and north elevations
and cross section, and plan of service
areas

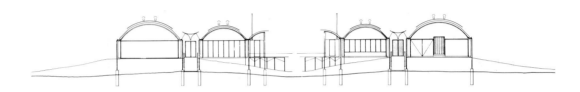

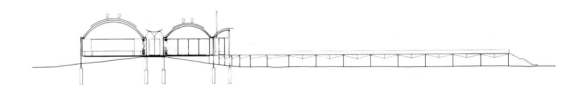

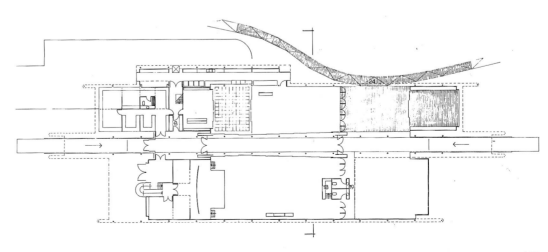

Elevations and cross sections of the
residences for the patients and their
families

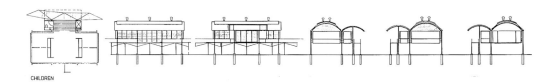

CHILDREN

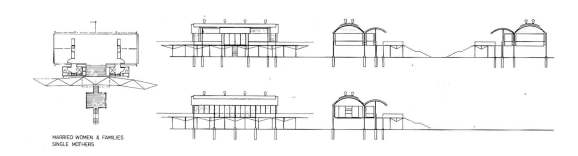

MARRIED WOMEN & FAMILIES
SINGLE MOTHERS

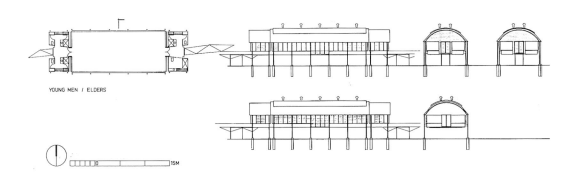

YOUNG MEN / ELDERS

0   15M

Minerals and Mining Museum (Project)
Broken Hill, New South Wales
1987–89

Broken Hill is an isolated desert mining town, close to the western border of New South Wales, where vast deposits of zinc, silver and lead have been mined for over a hundred years. Out of a long, narrow block in the town centre, the local authority wanted to create a museum to commemorate the mine and its former activities. After interviews with eight Australian architects, Murcutt was chosen.

Murcutt envisaged the museum as a double metaphor: as an oasis, to establish a connection with the desert climate, in which the slightest trace of underground water generates life; and as the experience of the mine. An old pit-head frame symbolically marks the museum entrance at the north-east end. A large metallic hall some three hundred metres in length, the building houses two very different levels. The ground floor is essentially an enclosed box in which the exhibition route follows a straight line in semi-darkness, interrupted regularly by the intense penetration of light through slits in the walls. Murcutt wanted to re-create the visual sensation of descending into a mine shaft, in which the lift alternately passes opaque geological layers and brightly lit galleries. The first floor, on the other hand, is completely open beneath a metal umbrella-like roof. The structure's wide overhang on the north side protects the façade from the vertical summer sunlight, and its backward tilt allows the sun's low rays to penetrate in winter. It also permits the huge machines on display to be seen from outside. Water in the outside pond reflects light on to the underside of the roof.

Despite the dry and burning summer temperatures, the museum is designed to function without air conditioning. On the ground floor, thick,

rammed earth walls (.8 and .5 metres on the north and south sides, respectively), built from the site's red earth, act as a thermal screen. They are fitted with *malqafs* – wind traps attached to fountains in old Cairo houses – that ventilate and cool the interior. Murcutt can thus keep the temperature in the exhibition rooms at around 23°C, some 10°C lower than outside. He also placed crushed aromatic plants in the *malqafs* so that the air is scented with desert fragrances. Simulations by the Victoria Technology Centre using a plexiglass model and blowers confirmed the expected functioning of the building's air currents.

For financial reasons the building, which has a total surface area of three thousand square metres, was to be built in two stages, The metal frames were to be prefabricated in Sydney and taken to Broken Hill by lorry. Phase 1 (at a cost of $2.1A million) was ready for execution, but the project was abandoned in 1989.

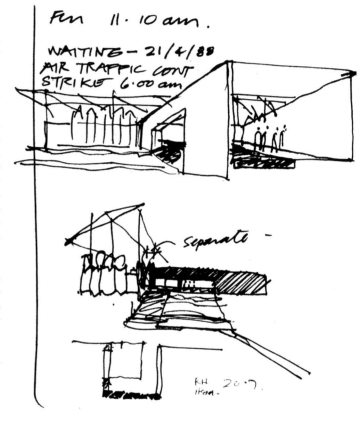

Cross sections and views from the
north-east, north-west and south-east
fronts, and plans of the two levels

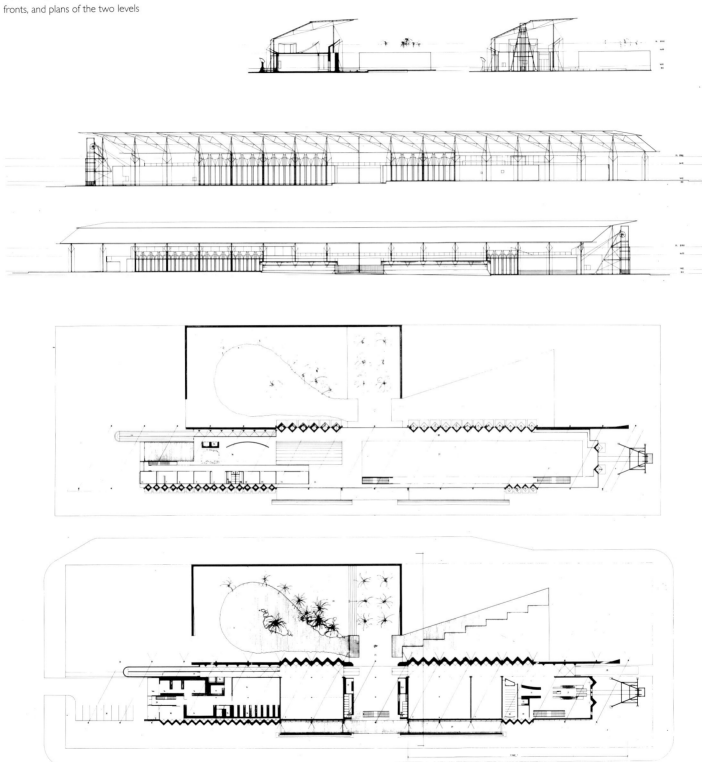

Sketch of the north-west façade and model

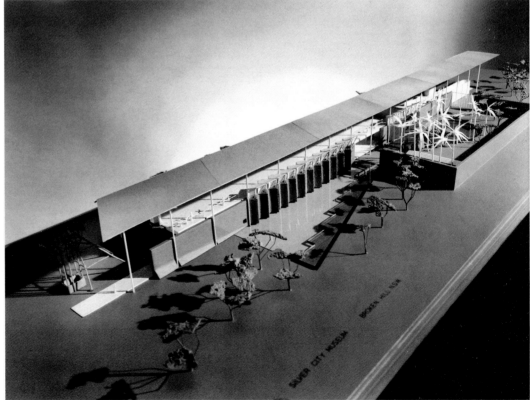

Sketch of the north end of the museum and a model

23/5/86

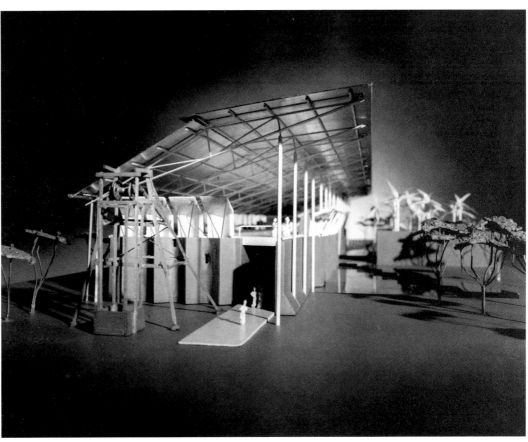

Magney House
Paddington, Sydney
1986–90

For the clients of the Bingi Point house, who wanted a town house with the same qualities of openness to the elements, Murcutt effectively transformed a terrace house in the historic Paddington quarter near central Sydney. The great achievements of this project lie in its deft use of light and of the views.

The site itself was extremely constrictive: a narrow site that sloped sharply north between a street and an alley; two long, blind party walls; obligation to conserve the listed street façade and respect the outline of the building. Murcutt therefore treated the fourth façade as a large window for the entire house. He designed a vertical terrace projecting into the garden and contained by walls with bevelled ends. The terrace captures the north light, frames the landscape and provides privacy from the sides.

The interior was entirely reconstructed. Murcutt literally cut the ground floor in two, raising the garden side containing the main bedroom sixty centimetres above the street side, where one enters. He thus created a visual connection between garden and street entrance that permits the movement of air and light from one façade to the other across the lower floor. This ploy also allows almost the entire interior volume to be seen from any standpoint. The entrance lighting is supplemented by a small window on the street side and a band of skylights.

Circulation is along the west party wall, while the utility areas and services are along the east wall. The garden level is a single open-plan room extending from the entrance in the customary sequence – kitchen, dining room, sitting room. The structural

and visual interrelationship of the three levels is exposed in elegant six-metre cruciform beams that support the roof and bedroom storey from the living room. The floor is entirely tiled in grey stone pavers, and the ceilings are lined with white ripple iron; the furniture is by Alvar Aalto and Arne Jacobsen.

The living area can be extended on to the terrace and garden by opening up huge glazed pivoting metal doors (2.7 x 4 metres). The terrace can thus be transformed into an outside living area shaded by a removable sailcloth awning, plaited in layers to vary the density of the light. The colour of the walls was chosen to reflect the Australian desert.

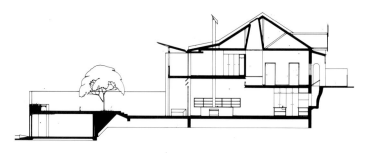

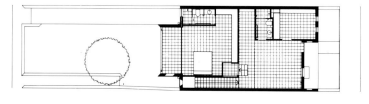

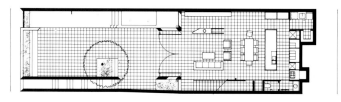

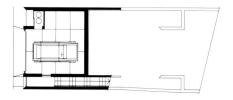

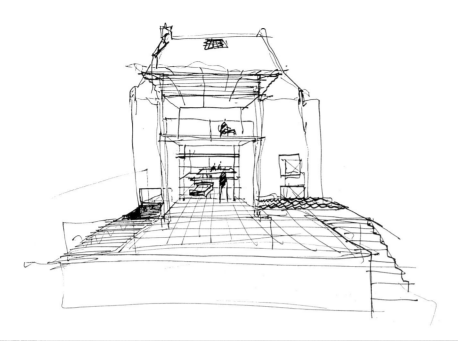

Perspective sktech and views of the veranda and the pool

Sketch and view of the living room
which leads on to the veranda

Sketch and view of the dining area and kitchen with stairs leading to the first floor

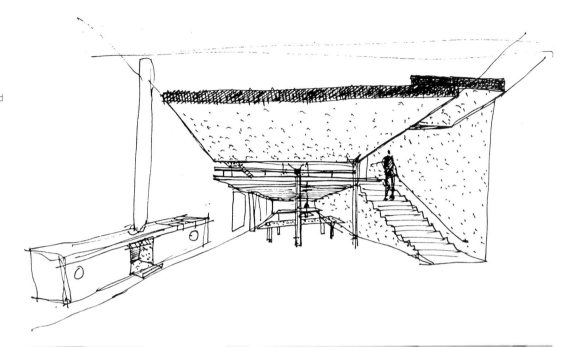

Done House
Mosman, Sydney
1988–91

Sketch of the west façade and views of the house's elevation overlooking the bay and its east façade

Perspective sketch and view of the internal courtyard (opposite)

Mosman is a comfortable suburb on Middle Harbour, one of the inlets of Sydney Harbour. At the corner of an avenue and a footpath to Chinaman's Beach lies the Done house, on a site sloping sharply to the north and commanding an outstanding sea view. Ken Done is a Sydney-based artist well-known for his paintings and drawings, and Murcutt had already renovated his previous house in 1978, as well as converted an old bungalow on the beach below this house into a studio.

For this project Murcutt wanted to abstract the intimacy of the house from the neighbouring buildings. Three of the façades are solid brick, broken only by occasional apertures that from the interior frame select vistas of vegetation. Only the north façade opens fully to the sun and the panorama. The house comprises two pavilions that are staggered in line with the slope and laterally served on three storeys by a series of staircases grouped against the east (footpath) façade. Entrance is from the top floor, which leads down to the living areas via a high-ceilinged skylit corridor that also serves as a picture gallery. The lower floor is devoted to the children. On the middle (and principal) storey, the north pavilion's living room and the parents' bedroom in the south pavilion flank an inner courtyard that brings the bay views far back into the house. The courtyard is a static composition with white walls, a pool and a frangipani, at once reminiscent of Greek islands, the work of Luis Barragán and David Hockney's California paintings. A straight staircase leads up from the courtyard to a sun terrace.

The two almost symmetrical metal frames of the tall north façade correspond to the living room's veranda and the dining room's loggia. The gallery façade and roof are fitted with electric Venetian blinds for controlling natural light and ventilation. Murcutt also introduced glazed slits in the corners of the courtyard and oblique embrasures to permit diagonal vistas and give the interior space more fluidity. The Mediterranean feeling is emphasized by the client's choice of flooring – large terracotta tiles – and colours – pure white throughout the interior, with yellow ochre outside.

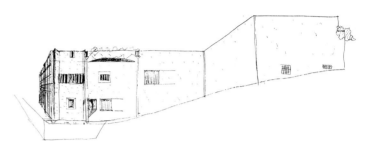

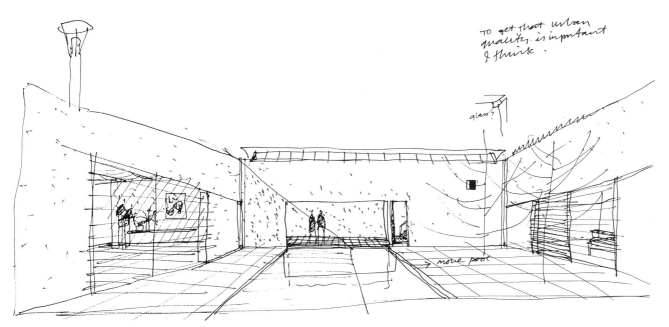

To get that urban quality is important I think.

glass?

→ move pool

Details of the drainpipe, west-
elevation drawing and cross sections
through the courtyard

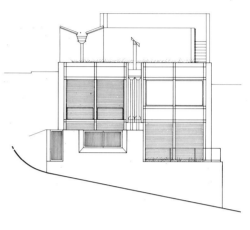

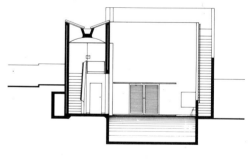

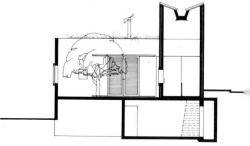

Plans of the three floors, east and south
elevation drawings and longitudinal cross
section

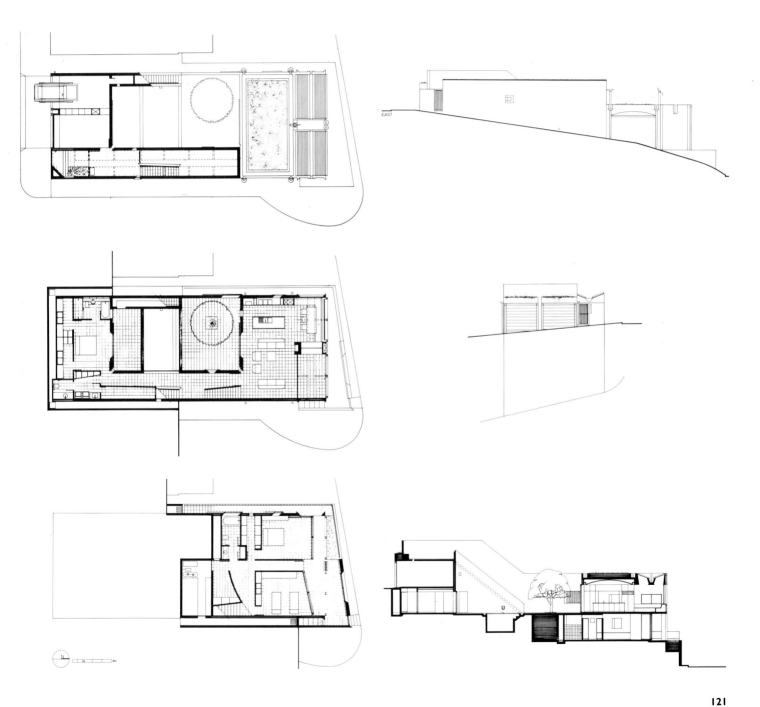

Views of the courtyard from the
solarium, corridor, staircase leading to
the solarium

Muston House
Seaforth, Sydney
1988–92

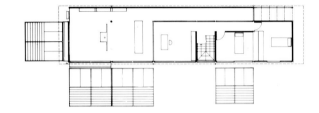

This site, an ordinary plot on Sydney's Middle Harbour, was already occupied by a large bungalow when Murcutt took on the commission. The deep indentation in the side of road was created because the new house was built behind the existing residence, where the clients lived during construction. Following their move into the new pavilion, the old bungalow was removed by crane without being demolished, and taken by lorry to its new location. Only the garage remains.

Following the slope of the ground and maintaining the mandatory distance of 0.9 metres from the property line, the house is arranged over three long and narrow storeys. The lowest, at street level, is the boathouse. The next, 2.5 metres above the street level and flush with the back garden, contains the main living space, the family room. The first floor has children's bedrooms and a mezzanine above the family room. The double-height space extends laterally and longitudinally on to tiled platforms that are protected by sailcloth awnings – 'sails' that direct the north-east breezes into the house's interior.

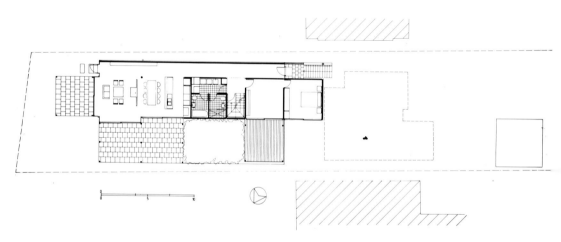

A sketch of the longitudinal section and
views of the paved external spaces and
canvas awnings

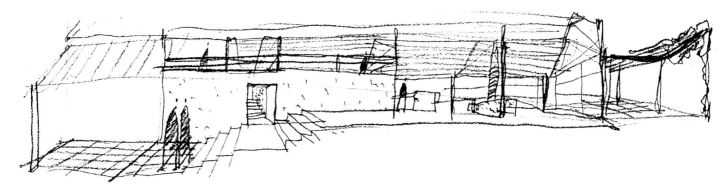

Perspective sketch and views of the
living area/kitchen

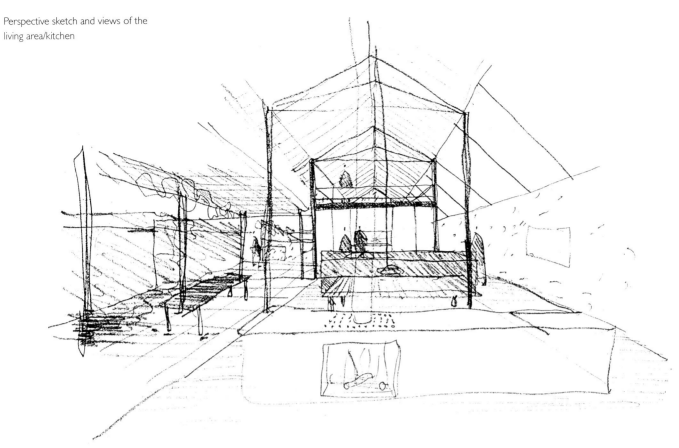

Pratt House
Kew, Melbourne
1983–94

Pratt House is the extension of Raheen, the former residence of the Archbishop of Melbourne dating from 1884. The new owners, active patrons of the arts and public benefactors, wanted to build a new house for themselves and keep Raheen for entertaining. They wanted a luminous, transparent dwelling that would resemble the conservatories of grand 19th-century residences and counterpoint the heavy brick construction and dark rooms of the existing mansion. The two houses were to be linked and capable of functioning as a single building. Murcutt was chosen for the project from a host of Australian and American architects. The restoration of Raheen was entrusted to the oldest firm of architects in Melbourne, Bates, Smart, McCutcheon, who also acted as associates architects for the new building.

Apart from the existing building, the site is characterized by its panoramic view over its surroundings to the north. Murcutt designed a large glazed pavilion behind Raheen, level with it on one side, towering above the view on the other. The new building encloses the u-shaped plan of Raheen's three wings, creating a courtyard between the reception room in the old building and the living room in the new. He retained the old house's ceiling heights to calibrate the two structures' proportions and to allow a functional continuity between the buildings through two points of contact: the Raheen library and dining room, which are linked, respectively, to the new pavilion's living room and kitchen. The kitchen has its own entrance, independent from Raheen's grand entrance.

The principle of distribution recalls that of the Littlemore house: two residential floors, with the living room on the ground level and the bedrooms above, divided into parents' and children's accommodations on either side of an empty space; passageways and service blocks are grouped in a high gallery on the south side. The house rests on a massive base that contains all the mechanical services rooms, with a curving supporting wall faced in grey stone. The metal skeleton is composed of a series of frames with cruciform columns in composite welded sections. In the eastern half of the house, these frames are set 4.8 metres apart, at right angles to the main body of Raheen; the frame's module increases toward the west gable, where it fans out to come into parallel with the stables. Large ribbed cast concrete tiles resting on gondola-shaped beams (with a span of 8 metres) make up the first-storey floor, which is elevated 5.2 metres above the ground. Beams and ribbing are left exposed below, like the warp and weft of a fabric – an effect underscored by the contrast in their colours. The roof is covered in zinc.

All the façades are glazed. The north façade is shielded from the sun by a series of tinted laminated-glass awnings. The highest, an extension of the roof, protects the large pivoting glazed panels on the bedroom façade. These panels project over the awning below them, which in turn protects the living room's large sliding doors. This sculptural display of the metal structure and the awnings' scaly glass carapace give the house's exterior the appearance of an immobile, articulated insect.

The Pratt house occupies a place of its own in Murcutt's oeuvre. First, it

marks a radical departure from the modest scale of his earlier domestic projects, costing more than $10A million. Second, Murcutt succumbed to the use of technological methods, artificial ventilation (air conditioning, not louvres, at the client's request) and the most advanced building techniques: glazing with special qualities and dimensions, awnings that were measured and cut by laser, and electric hydraulic controls for opening the bedrooms' tilting partitions, developed by an aeronautical manufacturer. He demonstrates his dazzling talent for the expression of metal and highly worked details. Still, it is difficult to reconcile the scale imposed by the existing building and the clients' desire for transparency and grandeur in a program that is in effect an everyday house (one large living room and four bedrooms): the grand proportions and luxurious materials that attempt to resolve this dilemma give it the character of a small institutional building.

Preliminary sketches and the model of
the first project

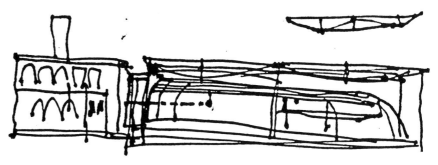

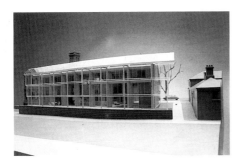

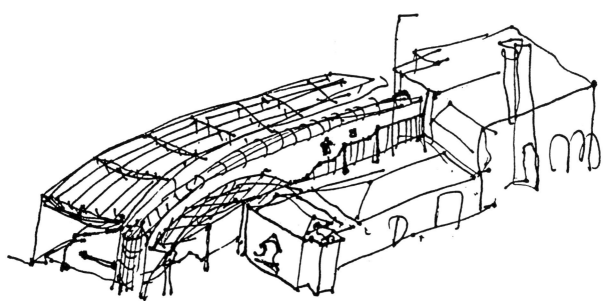

Cross section and a night view of the
north façcade

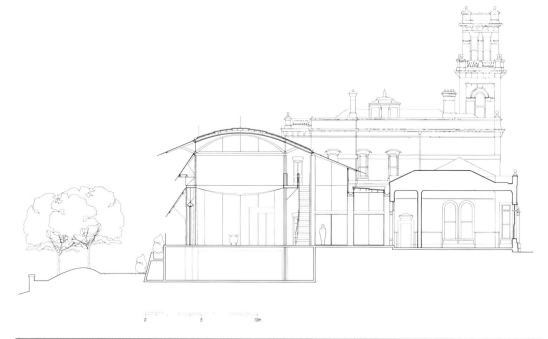

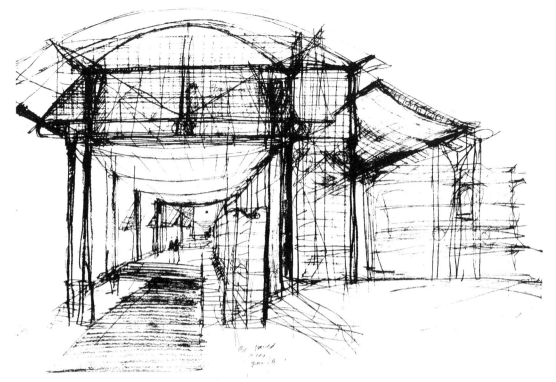

Sketch and view of the building's curved
section

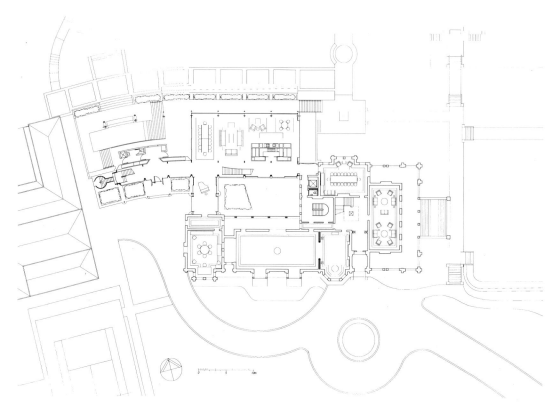

Ground-floor site plan and a view of
the pool

First-floor plan and interior details of the
extension

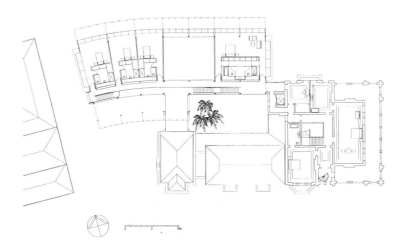

Meagher House
Bowral, New South Wales
1988–92

A hundred and fifty kilometres south of Sydney, between Bowral and Mittagong, the house's sloping site is on grassland forming part of an agricultural property and planted with a few magnificent eucalyptuses. It has fine northerly views towards Bowral from the crest and towards Mittagong below. Murcutt chose to position the house at the slope's foot to protect it from the occasionally violent south and south-westerly winds while preserving the ridge's natural outline.

He had already experimented with a similar arrangement of independent pavilions grafted on to either side of a circulatory passageway, notably in the Munro house at Bingara (1981–83). Here the passage is a continuation of the entrance path, which approaches from the road at a tangent to the site's contour. A workshop-garage and a study are sited at each end of the living areas. The construction system combines brick walls, roughly coated in red ochre pigment on the exterior, with a silvery metal frame that supports the large roof. All the living rooms face north, and their clerestory windows form a long screen that reflects the eucalyptuses' foliage. Views are isolated and framed by the openings, straight or oblique, which can be screened by adjusting the wooden shutters. The slightly elevated courtyard allows the farm animals to graze in the area around the house without fencing. The residence has a certain autonomy from urban utility services: it has its own septic tank and corrugated-iron watertanks with a maximum capacity of 33,000 litres.

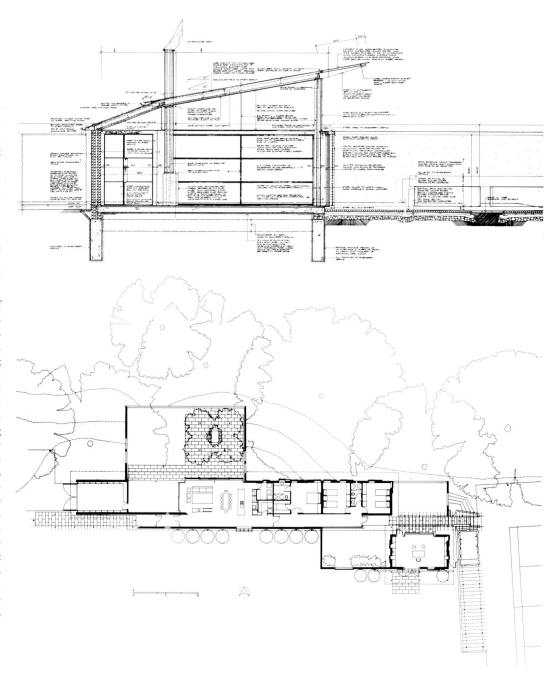

1:500 N/S SECTION

Sketch for the effects of wind and sunlight, and views of the back of the house with the water tanks and of the west façade

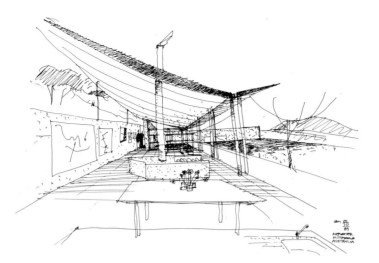

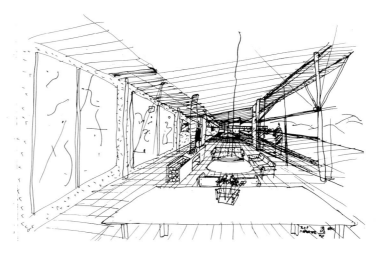

Interior perspective and views, and a
view of the veranda

Simpson-Lee House
Mount Wilson, New South Wales
1989–94

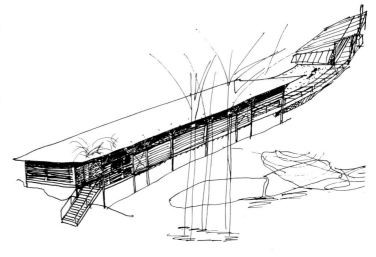

With demanding clients, a spartan program (a sanctuary for a retired couple of intellectual bent seeking withdrawal from the world), a magnificent site in the Blue Mountains (150 kilometres north-west of Sydney) comprising two isolated plots and some three hectares in total, a rich variety of flora, and an extraordinary panorama of hills and forests, the conception and realization of this project took nearly six years.

Backing on to the west and southwest winds, the house faces to the views of the east and north-east. Following the rocky massif that impedes extension to the rear, the residence's two pavilions stand on either side of a pond in a linear sequence. Murcutt designed the plan as a striking horizontal progression from the access path to the house. The path skirts the smaller studio pavilion, re-emerges as a walkway down the length of the pool, crosses the residential pavilion, and finally escapes down the stairway on the east side. As the path progresses, the ground beneath it slopes away, so that the house gets further and further from the ground. This dramatizes the progression and accentuates the sense of gradual detachment from the world sought by the inhabitants, allowing Murcutt to terminate the building with a fine isolated vertical member.

In the residential pavilion, the living room is symmetrically flanked by two vestibules and two bedroom suites on either side of the kitchen, which is reduced to a long strip of appliances. In the passage along the principal façade Murcutt reversed his customary plan: the bedrooms, tucked under the lowest part of the roof, have intimate proportions and very controlled light penetration. The north-east façade is relatively dense owing to the interplay of six glazed bays, the sliding insect screens and balustrades; the electrically operated aluminium Venetian blinds are guided by steel braces that are tapered and lightened by perforations. With the exception of the solid wood steps on the staircase and walkway, the house is wholly mineral: silver-painted steel and aluminium for the structure, casings and large sloping planes of the roofs; pale grey polished concrete on the floors; whitewash on all brick and plasterwork; and glass. The construction system and main façade are similar to those of the Meagher house; the back façade's sloping glass panes and ventilation slats recall the Bingi house.

The pressure from his clients pushed Murcutt to the limit of his architectural principles. The spare design, simplified to its utmost, is almost monastic. The strongly articulated longitudinal passage incorporates the elements in the landscape as much as leads though the living spaces, turning it into the building's raison d'être. The crystalline legibility of the spaces, barring only the two hidden bedroom units, asserts the role of the principal actor: the site. The house also confirms Murcutt's evolution towards a sort of abstract expressionist façade – a precious ribbed screen that responds to the rhythms of the great trees filtering the sun and the view.

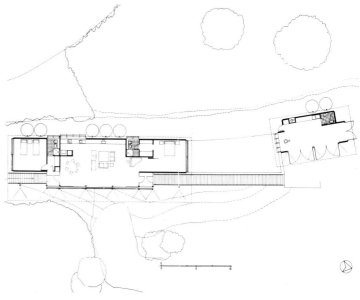

An end-on view of the studio and pool,
views of the main pavilion containing the
living area and staircase access, and an
interior view of the living area

Marika-Alderton House
Yirrkala Community, Eastern Arnhem Land, Northern Territory
1991–94

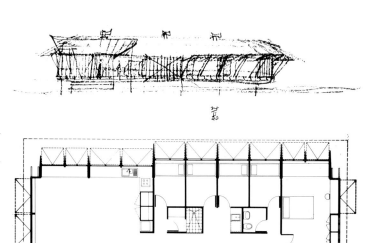

In the design of a house for an Aboriginal artist and her family Murcutt faced several new problems. First, he had to adapt to northern Australia's tropical climate; to submit his system of construction and detailing to the constraints of prefabrication because of the limited budget and the site's location in a remote area lacking in local skills; and to test his own spatial principles within the Aboriginal way of life, which he had used as a reference without actually realizing a project for any of their communities. In short, he had to 'build a bridge between the cultures'. He designed an elegant and sturdy long hall, which opens, closes and breathes like a plant.

The metal structure is built to resist winds with speeds of up to sixty-three metres per second. Compliance with anti-cyclone regulations resulted in the generous diameter of the columns and the wide struts bolted down at the junctions with the purlins. The house is entirely built without glass. According to their orientation and the nature of the rooms, the façades are composed of broad plywood or slatted tallow-wood shutters with eight millimetre gaps. During the daytime, these tilting panels are raised like awnings so the house becomes a sheltered platform, partly open on every side. At night the walls are closed again; thus the natural cross-ventilation remains constant, while the interior's intimacy is preserved. The roof has a wide overhang on the north façade (the entrance façade, looking on to the sea) to cover the platform's narrow projection along the length of the living room. On the south side Murcutt expanded his idea of a 'serving wall' to include the alcove beds in the bed-rooms, which are two metres above floor level for privacy. The alcoves are separated by vertical plywood fins that prevent the morning and evening sunrays from reaching the outer wall. Inside, plywood partitions are solid up to a height of two metres, and fitted above with lathing for ventilation; the pivoting venturi tubes punctuating the roof's ridge expel rising hot air.

The house was entirely prefabricated by a team of carpenters in Gosford, near Sydney, carried across Australia by lorry, then assembled *in situ* in a few weeks by just two craftsmen. The rigorous repetition of refined details and the builders' expertise in boat construction led to a perfectly crafted result. The steel manufacturer BHP donated the metal parts, and the architect and his engineer relinquished their fees to aid in the project's realization. The house is intended to be a prototype for a lightweight and economical dwelling, an alternative to the brick bungalows with small windows that are typically built for the Aborigines by the Australian authorities.

The Marika house returns to the spareness and simplicity of Murcutt's long country pavilions. In virtually abandoning the traditional notion of a façade, however, he explores the subtle and changing relationship of interior and exterior with renewed vigour, taking to new limits the idea of a changeable shelter in symbiosis with the landscape and natural elements. This ambiguity of outside and inside, largely dictated by climatic factors, engendered the most surprising feature of the project: the didactic expression of the relationship between frame, roof and walls, which in this case are treated like a skeleton and skin – an 'organic' manner that breaks away from the usual smoothness and fluidity of Murcutt's interiors.

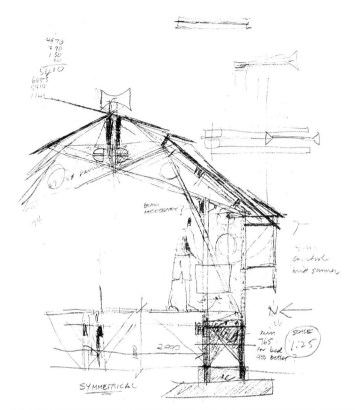

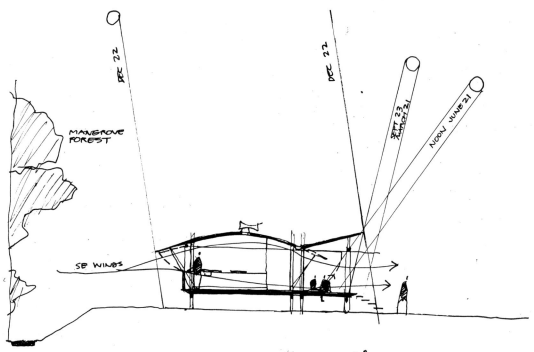

MANGROVE FOREST

DEC 22

DEC 22

SEPT 23 MARCH 21

NOON JUNE 21

SE WINDS

SECTION - LATITUDE 12½° S
LONGITUDE 137

A study of a section with notes on the effects of wind and sunlight and details showing the walls' ribbed panels and the roof structure

Sketch of the interior

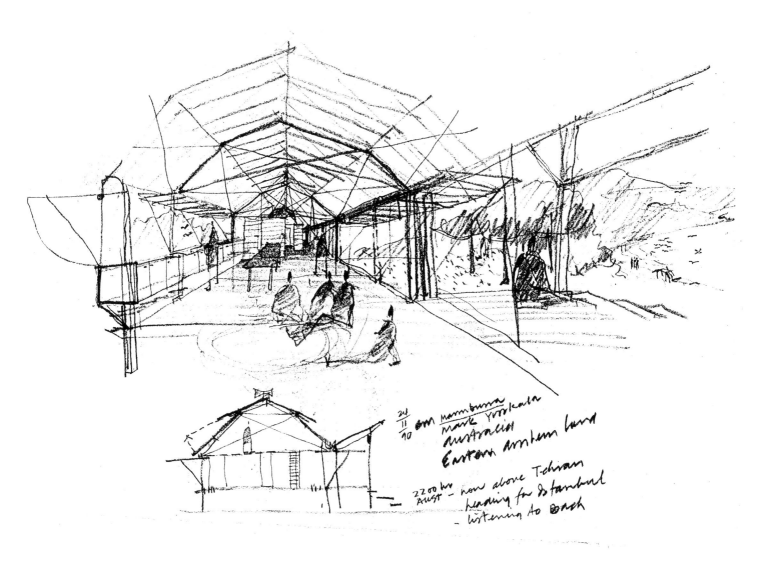

24/11/90 8am Marmburra
Mark Yirrkala
Australia
Eastern Arnhem Land

2200 hr — now above T-chran
AUST — heading for Istanbul
— listening to Bach

145

Interior and exterior views showing
details of the wall panels

Murcutt Guest Studio
Kempsey, New South Wales
1992

This small summer pavilion was constructed from an existing timber shed near Murcutt's farmhouse (formerly the Marie Short farmhouse) as a self-contained guest studio. It incorporates wood reclaimed from the pergola beside the main house during its previous ownership.

Murcutt renovated the shed, closed off its ends and added a number of service features: a veranda that extends the building's main body on the north side, and a facilities block on the west, both of which are covered by tilted roofs. There is also a gently sloping ramp to the entrance, and next to it is a small covered platform that provides direct access to the studio's living area through a large sliding door. On the exterior, the living accommodation and facilities are distinguished by wood and corrugated-iron cladding, respectively.

The interior's rustic simplicity (the exposure of the structure's elements); the contrast of old and new (the shed's sun-bleached wood, the frame's metal and the aluminium sliding doors); the architect's manifest delight in the elaboration of perfectly controlled details (the shower and its corner window open to the trees); the apparent casualness, in reality carefully contrived (unconcealed water heater and gas cylinders); the furniture and fittings (Artek, a stove imported from Denmark) – all contribute to an elegance reminiscent of many summer houses in the forests of Scandinavia.

Side view with access ramp and plan

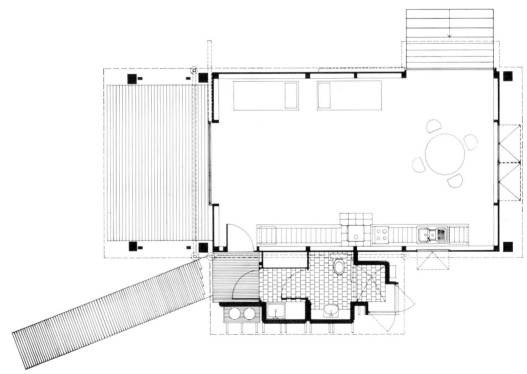

Detail of the entrance and of the living-room louvres

Interior views of the living area

Landscape Interpretation Centre
Kakadu National Park, Northern Territory
1992–1994

The Landscape Interpretation Centre is shown here in its design stage. This building is sited in a national park in northern Australia (originally a sacred Aboriginal site) as an extension to the existing building. The tropical climate and its constraints (extreme heat and humidity, the need for anti-cyclone protection) and the site's rocky escarpments helped shape Murcutt's plans as much as the program itself.

The project is based on an analysis of the local Aborigines' relationship with the territory, of which it sets out to be a metaphor. Murcutt's design explorations developed around several themes. The exhibition areas and little amphitheatre are gathered under a huge wing-like awning and bounded on the two longitudinal façades by screen-walls. The tour of the building moves in a loop ('a journey without beginning or end'), around and within an opaque core ('initiation'), between the mud walls ('refuge'), and opens to the surroundings ('prospect'). A planted pond is placed along the route ('it immediately translates the season, the rains, the drought'). The natural cross-ventilation was calculated to provide unaided cooling of the interior.

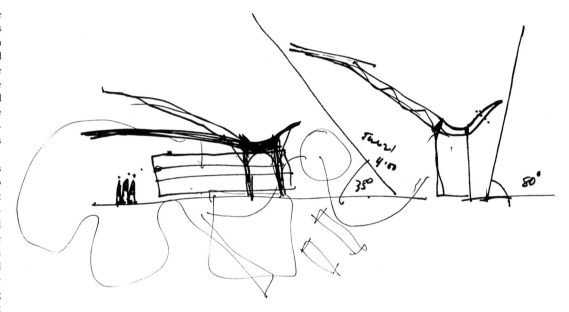

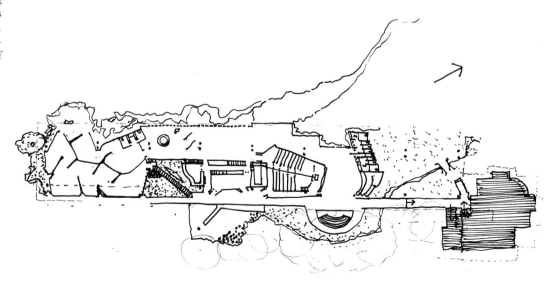

Perspective and model

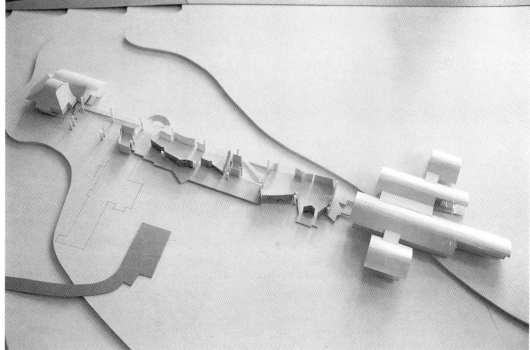

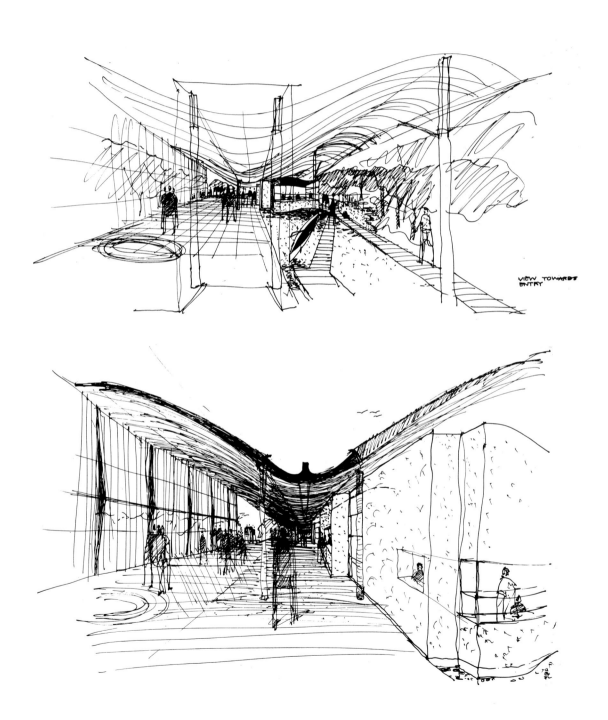

VIEW TOWARDS
ENTRY

Appendix

Biographical Notes

1936–

Born in London on 25 July, while his Australian parents are on a visit to Europe.

Lives in Upper Watut, Papua New Guinea, until 1941, then in Sydney, on the north bank of the harbour where he still lives and works today.

1956–61

Studies at Sydney Technical College, part of the University of New South Wales, Sydney. Diploma awarded 31 December 1961.

Works with various firms: Levido & Baker (1956), Neville Gruzman (1958–59) and Allen & Jack (1962).

1962–64

Spends a period in London. Works with the firm Ian Frazer & Associates.

Travels in Europe to Italy, Yugoslavia, Greece, France, Holland, Germany, Poland, Denmark, Sweden and Finland.

1964

Returns to Sydney. Works with the firm Ancher, Mortlock, Murray & Woolley.

1969

Founds the Glenn Murcutt firm.

1970–78

Design tutor at the University of Sydney.

1973

Second trip abroad ('world tour'), to Mexico, the United States, France, Great Britain, Spain and Italy.

1974–85

Receives nine awards (Blacket, Wilkinson and Sulman awards) from the Royal Australian Institute of Architects of the State of New South Wales.

1975–90

Lectures in the universities of the major Australian cities.

1982

Takes part in the Paris Biennale.

1982–85

Receives two Robin Boyd National Awards and the Zelman Cowan Commendation of the RAIA.

1983

Third trip abroad, to France, Spain, Morocco, Great Britain and the United States.

1985

Visiting Professor, University of New South Wales, Sydney.

1986

Fourth trip abroad, to the United States, Mexico, Great Britain and France.

1987

Travels to the United States and lectures in Mexico.

1988

Lectures at the Institute of Architecture, Auckland, New Zealand.

Lectures at the RAIA symposium 'Reflections'.

Serves on jury awarding prizes for residential accommodation on behalf of AIA/*Sunset Magazine* Western Division.

1989

Travels to Europe: lectures in Denmark (Danish Institute of Architects, Copenhagen and Institute of Architecture, Aarhus); in Norway (Oslo and Trondheim for the OAF); in Finland (public conference at Helsinki); in Britain (RIBA, London and in Winchester) and in Italy (University of Milan).

Guest critic of Masters of Architecture run by Haig Beck, Melbourne University.

1990

Travels to the United States: lectures at Austin University (TX); at the Rhode Island School of Design (RI); the symposium on education held by the ACSA and AIA at the Cranbrook Academy of Arts (MI).

Guest critic at the Graduate School of Fine Arts, School of Landscape Architecture, Philadelphia (PA).

Travels to France invited by the Mission Interministérielle des Grands Travaux to sit on the jury judging the competition held for the Kanaka Cultural Centre in Nouméa, New Caledonia.

1990–92

Visiting Professor at the University of Technology, Sydney.

1991

Travels to Nouméa, New Caledonia, to sit on the jury for the competition held for the Kanaka Cultural Centre.

Two trips to the United States: lectures at the College of Architecture, University of Arizona, Tucson and Taliesin West (AZ); at Pomona University and the University of San Luis Obispo (CA); at the University of New Mexico, Albuquerque (NM); at Harvard University Graduate School of Design (MA); at the University of Virginia, Charlottesville (VA); at the Architectural League and the Parsons School of Design, New York (NY).

In Canada, lectures at the Architectural League of Vancouver.

Takes part in the Venice Biennale.

1991–95

Adjunct Professor at the School of Landscape Architecture, Graduate School of Fine Arts, Philadelphia (PA).

1992

RAIA Gold Medal 1992, received in June in Sydney.

Seventh Alvar Aalto Medal received in October in Helsinki (Finland).

Buildings and Projects

Dates refer to those on approved working drawings

1960

Devitt house, Beacon Hill, Sydney (completed 1962; since altered)

1968

Daphne Murcutt house, Seaforth, Sydney (several projects, 1968, 1971–72)
Glenn Murcutt house, Mosman, Sydney (alteration/addition; completed 1969; since altered)
Glenn Murcutt house, Beauty Point, Sydney (project, 1968–70)

1969

Douglas Murcutt house, Belrose, Sydney (completed 1972)

1970

Robertson house, East Killara, Sydney (alteration/addition; since altered)
Hinder house, Gordon, Sydney (alteration/addition to a Syd Ancher house)

1971

Lowy house, Mosman, Sydney
Walker house, Killara, Sydney (alteration/addition to a Syd Ancher house)

1972

Needham house, Woy Woy, Sydney (in association with Guy Maron)
Restaurant Paragon, Katoomba, New South Wales (renovation)
Omega Project house for Ralph Symonds Homes
Laurie Short house, Terrey Hills, Sydney (completed in 1973)
Cullen house, Balmain, Sydney (completed in 1974)
Armstrong house, Grenfell, New South Wales (completed in 1980)

1973

Luscombe house, Bayview, Sydney
Wallis house, Manly, Sydney (renovation/addition)

1974

Marie Short house, Kempsey, New

South Wales (completed 1975)
Hetherton house, Balmain, Sydney (completed 1982)

1975

Jureidini house, Mosman, Sydney (alteration/addition of Murcutt's former house)
Meehan house, Kempsey, New South Wales (completed 1977)
Redmond house, Giralang, Canberra (completed 1977)

1976

Stitt house, Longueville, New South Wales (alteration/addition 1977)
Done house, Mosman, Sydney (alteration/addition; completed 1978)

1977

Ockens house, Cromer, Sydney (completed 1978)
Reynolds house, Woollahra, Sydney (completed 1979)
Nicholas house, Mount Irvine, New South Wales (completed 1980)
Berowra Waters Inn, Sydney (phase 1, completed 1978)

1978

Young house, Jindabyne, New South Wales (alteration/addition, completed 1980; since altered)
Carruthers farmhouse, Mount Irvine, New South Wales (completed 1980)

1979

Project house for Devon-Symonds Pty Ltd, North Rocks, New South Wales
Isherwood house, Mosman, Sydney (alteration/addition; since altered)
Hawksford, Point Piper, Sydney (project)
Nielsen Park Kiosk, Vaucluse, Sydney (project)
Crouch house, Cobbity, Sydney (in association with Wendy Lewin and Alex Tzannes; project)
Offices for Marsh & Freedmann, Woolloomooloo, Sydney (conversion, completed 1980; since altered)
Hornery house, Warrawee, Sydney (in association with Civil & Civic, completed 1982)

1980

Competition for the renovation of the 'Engehurst' villa designed by the architect John Verge, in association with the conference 'Pleasures of Architecture' organized by the RAIA, Sydney
Markovic house, Palm Beach, Sydney (in association with Wendy Lewin and Alex Tzannes; project)
Fountain house, McMahons Point, Sydney
Uther house, Hunters Hill, Sydney (in association with Wendy Lewin and Alex Tzannes)
Murcutt-Robertson house, Kempsey (extension to Marie Short house)
Carpenter house, Point Piper, Sydney (completed 1982)
Zachary's Restaurant, Terrey Hills, Sydney (completed 1983)
Ball-Eastaway house and studio, Glenorie, Sydney (Graham Jahn and Rad Milatich, assistants; Alex Tzannes, site visits; completed 1983)

1981

Ward house, Hornsby Heights, Sydney (project)
Maestri house, Blueys Beach, New South Wales
Museum of Local History and Tourist Office, Kempsey, New South Wales (phase 1, completed 1982)
Fredericks house, Jamberoo, New South Wales (Wendy Lewin, assistant; completed 1982)
New Catholic Presbytery and Community Hall, Mona Vale, Sydney (Graham Jahn, assistant; completed 1983)
Munro house, Bingara, New South Wales (Graham Jahn, assistant; completed 1983)
Rabbit house, Merewether, New South Wales (Graham Jahn, assistant; completed 1983)

1982

Ramsden & Kee house, Blackheath, New South Wales (completed 1983)
Newport house, Hunters Hill, Sydney (addition)
Berowra Waters Inn, Sydney (phase 2; Graham Jahn, assistant; completed 1983)
Magney house, Bingi Point, Sydney (completed 1984)

1983

Finlay house, Hallidays Point, New South Wales (John Smith, assistant; Alex Tzannes, site visits; completed 1984)
Littlemore house, Woollahra, Sydney (Wendy Lewin, assistant; completed 1986)
Aboriginal Alcoholic Rehabilitation Centre, Bennelong's Haven, Kinchela Creek, New South Wales (project, 1983–85)
Pratt house, extension of Raheen, Kew, Melbourne (in association with Melbourne architects Bates, Smart & McCutcheon; completed 1994)

1985

Edwards-Neil house, Lindfield, New South Wales (project, 1985–88)
Herbarium and Visitors Centre, Botanical Gardens, Wollongong, New South Wales (project)

1986

Field Study Centre, Cape Tribulation, Far North Queensland (project, 1986–87)
Harrison house, Waverley, Sydney (in association with Alex Tzannes; phase 1 completed 1989; phase 2 completed 1991)
Magney house, Paddington, Sydney (renovation; James Grose, site assistant; Andrew McNally and Sue Barnsley, landscape architects; completed 1990)

1987

Carey house, Springwood, New South Wales
Minerals and Mining Museum, Broken Hill, New South Wales (project, 1987–89; Reg Lark, assistant)
Museum of Local History, Kempsey, New South Wales (phase 2, completed 1988)
Cultural Centre for the University of North Solomon, Arawa, Papua New Guinea (project, 1987–88)
Offices for Marsh & Freedman, Redfern, Sydney (renovation/conversion, completed 1989)

1988

Done house, Mosman, Sydney (Reg Lark, assistant; completed 1991)

Meagher house, Bowral, New South
    Wales (Andrea Wilson, assistant; James
    Grose, site assistant; completed 1992)
Muston house, Seaforth, Sydney
    (completed 1992)

1989

Simpson-Lee house, Mount Wilson, New
    South Wales (completed 1994)

1991

Marika-Alderton house, Yirrkala
    Community, Eastern Arnhem Land,
    Northern Territory (completed 1994)

1992

Preston house, St Ives, Sydney (Sue
    Barnsley, landscape architect; completed
    1994)
Landscape Interpretation Centre, National
    Park of Kakadu, Northern Territory (in
    association with Troppo Architects,
    Darwin; completed 1994)
Murcutt guest studio, Kempsey, New
    South Wales

1993–95, projects in progress:

Conversion of Customs house (architects:
    Mortimer Lewis, James Barnet, Walter
    Liberty Vernon, then George
    Oakschott), Circular Quay, Sydney (in
    association with Wendy Lewin)
Williams house, Pearl Beach, New South
    Wales
Douglas Murcutt house, Woodside, South
    Australia
Furman house, Stirling, South Australia
Olsen house, Norton Summit, South
    Australia
Killman house, Copacabana, New South
    Wales
Chambers house, Turamurra, Sydney
Ken and Judy Done Gallery, Mosman,
    Sydney
Funston house, Northbridge, Sydney
Hardeman-McGrath house, Birchgrove,
    Sydney (extension, with Nicholas
    Murcutt)
Taylor house, Barrington Tops, New
    South Wales

Bibliography

Entries are given in chronological order

A.L. Morgan, C. Naylor, *Contemporary Architects* (no date). 'Devitt House' in *Cross Section*, 134, December 1963, p.3.

H. Tanner, *Australian Housing in the Seventies*, Ure Smith, Sydney, 1976, pp.30–33.

'Ferme de Kempsey' in *Architecture Australia*, vol.66, 6, January 1978, p.58.

'House at Peacock Point' in *Architecture Australia*, vol.67, 6, January 1979, p.29.

M. Emmanuel, *Contemporary Architects*, Macmillan, London, 1980. 'The Competition of Engehurst' in *Architecture Australia*, vol. 69, 2, May 1980, pp.68–69.

I. McDougall, 'Glenn Murcutt's Houses' in *Transition*, vol.1, 4, October 1980, pp.33–35.

'Robin Boyd Award. Two houses, Mount Irvine, a sense of place' in *Architecture Australia*, vol.70, 6, December 1981, pp.10–13.

La modernité ou l'esprit du temps, catalogue of Paris Biennale, architectural section, L'Equerre, Paris, 1982, pp.214, 215.

A. Metcalf, 'Flashing forms of corrugated steel for week end farmers' in *AIA Journal*, August 1982, pp.62, 63.

J. Taylor, 'Revision of a corrugated iron tradition' in *A + U*, 11 November 1982, pp. 113–118.

'Wilkinson Award. Two houses, Mount Irvine' in *Architecture Australia*, vol.71, 6, December 1982, pp.14, 15.

L. Paroissien, M. Griggs, *Old continent, new building: contemporary Australian architecture*, David Ell Press & Design Arts Committee of Australian Council, Sydney, 1983.

'Jamberoo House' in *Architecture Australia*, vol.72, 3, May 1983, p.53.

'Museum and Tourist Information Centre, Kempsey' in *Architecture Australia*, vol.72, 7, December 1983, pp.8, 33.

J. Baird, *By Design: Changing Australian Housing*, AE Press, Melbourne, 1984.

P. Drew, 'Glenn Murcutt, museum, Kempsey, 1981' in *International Architect*, 4, 1984, pp.16, 17.

R. Spence, 'Museum Boundaries' in *Architectural Review*, vol.175, 1044, February 1984, pp.45–47.

P. Drew, 'Murcutt's metal vaults shelter a regional museum' in *AIA Journal*, September 1984, pp.188, 189.

'Museum and tourist information centre, Pacific Highway, South Kempsey' in *Builder NSW*, vol.13, 10, November 1984, pp.672–79.

'Ball-Eastaway residence,Glenorie' in *Architecture Australia*, vol.73, 8, December 1984, p.45.

P. Drew, *Leaves of Iron – Glenn Murcutt, Pioneer of an Australian Architectural Form*, The Law Book Company Limited, 1985.

C. McGregor, *Australian built – responding to place*, Design Art Board of the Australia Council, Sydney, 1985, pp.16, 17, 89.

'Museum and tourist office, Kempsey, 1983' in *Space Design*, 244, January 1985, pp.112–15.

'The Robin Boyd Award. House on the South Coast' in *Architecture Australia*, vol.74, 8, December 1985, pp.26–29.

R. Spence, 'House, Glenorie, near Sydney' and 'Offices, Wooloomooloo, Sydney' in *Architectural Review*, vol.178, 1066, December 1985, pp.30–37.

H.J. Cowan, *Encyclopedia of Building Technology*, Prentice Hall, New York, 1986.

R. Spence, 'At Bingie Point, house, Moruya, New South Wales' in *Architectural Review*, vol.179, 1068, February 1986, pp.70–75.

A. Truppin, 'Down by the river' in *Interiors*, 7, February 1986, pp.124–29.

M.H. Contal, 'Maisons, Glenorie et Moruya' in *Cree*, 210, February–March 1986, pp.82–89.

N.L. Hansen, A.D. Radford, 'Living on the edge: a grammar for some country houses by Glenn Murcutt' in *Architecture Australia*, vol.75, 5, July 1986, pp.66–73.

P. Drew, 'House like a butterfly spreading his wings' in *Architecture*, vol.75, 9, September 1986, Sydney, pp.58–60.

'Maintaining a link with Australian tradition' in *House and Garden*, vol.41, 10, October 1986, pp.122–25.

A. Ogg, *Architecture in steel – the Australian context*, RAIA, Canberra, 1987.

'Farmhouse at Jamberoo, Australia, 1981; two houses at Mt. Irvine, Australia,

1981' in *Space Design*, 268, January 1987, pp.92–95.

C. Pickering, 'Architettura e Australia secondo Glenn Murcutt' in *Casavogue*, 181, January 1987, special issue, pp.70–95.

'Welblech im hightech Design; Welblech für neue Erfahrungen' in *Architektur & Wohnen*, 3, June–July 1987, pp.104–17.

R. Spence, 'Murcutt goes to town' in *Architectural Review*, vol.182, 1085, July 1987, pp.53–57.

M. Dunworth, 'Natural Empathy' in *Belle*, 84, December 1987–January 1988, pp.68–76.

M. De Giorgi, 'House at Moruya, NSW, Australia' in *Domus*, 691, 1988, pp.68–75.

J.V. De Sousa, 'Realist architecture in the Australian idiom: the work of Glenn Murcutt' in *Center*, vol.4, pp.90–99.

H. Rasch, 'Kunstwerkstatt im Australischen Bush' in *Häuser*, 3, 1988, pp.114–21.

'Lavori privilegiati, luoghi privilegiati: nel bush australiano, un padiglione di lamiera' in *Abitare*, vol.264, May 1988, pp.191–99.

P. Goad, P. Tombesi, R. Vanucci, 'Architettura di lamiera' in *Spazio e società*, 43, July–September 1988, pp.60–77.

P. Drew, 'Touch-this-earth-lightly. Glenn Murcutt's unbuilt Aboriginal Alcoholic Rehabilitation Centre in *Architectural Review*, vol.184, 1100, October 1988, pp.91, 92.

P. Drew, K. Dirkinck, 'Murcutt og den australske regionalisme' in *Arkitekten*, vol.90, 18, October 1988, pp.438–48.

P. Tombesi, R. Vanucci, 'Architetture australiane' in *Casabella*, vol.52, 550, October 1988, pp.55–57.

T. Watkins, 'Glenn Murcutt, architect of integrity' in *Home and Building*, October–November 1988, pp.144–49.

'Farmhaus in Jamberoo, Australien' in *Detail*, 29, 1989, pp.16–19.

J. Dunn, 'Glenn Murcutt' in *On Design*, 1, 1989, pp.6–9.

J. Demos, 'Building in the country' in *Critiques*, 3, 1989, pp.93–96.

W.S. Ling, 'Notes on Glenn Murcutt's theoretical position – The rational

and the poetic', ibid. pp.97–102.

H. Lyon, 'Murcutt reconsidered', ibid. pp.89–92.

F. Vitelli, 'Nature–Object–Landscape', ibid. pp.78–88.

R. Spence, 'Court of Murcutt (office in Redfern, Sydney)' in *Architectural Review*, vol.185, 1105, March 1989, pp.87–91.

'Essence of the outback' in *Building Design* 933, 21, April 1989, pp.28, 29.

J. Pardey, 'Outback warrior' in *Building Design*, 934, 28 April 1989, p.2.

D. Dunster, *Key Buildings of the 20th Century – Houses 1945/89*, Butterworth Architecture, London, 1990.

R. Pegrum, *Details in Australian architecture no.1*, RAIA, Canberra, 1990.

H. Rasch, 'Ein Haus wurde lang und länger' in *Häuser*, 3, 1990, pp.32–37.

J. Taylor, *Australian architecture since 1960*, RAIA, Canberra, 1990.

P. Tombesi, 'Aboriginal alcoholic rehabilitation centre, Kinchela Creek' in *Spazio e società*, 49, January–March 1990, pp.102–5.

F. Fromonot, 'Glenn Murcutt: Maison, Kilminster Lane, Sydney' in *Cree*, 234 February 1990, pp.118–21.

R. Blunck, 'La maison du bout du monde' in *Journal de la Maison*, 235, March 1990, pp.46–53.

'Architetture per il sito; la casa nella campagna (Kempsey)' in *Abitare*, vol.284, April 1990, pp.154–63.

A.W. Spirn, 'Architecture in the landscape' in *Landscape architecture*, vol.80, 8, August 1990, pp.34–41.

M. Leccese, M. Anderson, 'Wanted: an earth-connected architecture', ibid. pp.64–67.

S. Amourgis (ed.), *Critical Regionalism*, The Pomona Meeting Proceedings, College of Environmental Design, California State Polytechnic University, Pomona 1991.

P. Freeman, J. Vulder (ed.), *The Australian Dwelling*, RAIA, Canberra, 1991, pp.47–54.

D. Sharp, *Dictionary of Architects and Architecture*, Quarto, London, 1991.

B. Vale, R. Vale, *Green Architecture. Design for a Sustainable Future*, Thames and Hudson, London, 1991.

'Image/Voyage' in *Archi Made*, 31, February 1991, pp.24–25.

'Glenn Murcutt, architect of the decade' in *Steel Profile*, 35, March 1991, special issue, p.9.

F. Fromonot, 'Maison Magney, Sydney' in *Cree*, 243, June–July 1991, pp.76–79.

R. Spence, 'Nature in the city' in *Architectural Review*, vol.189, 1134, August 1991, pp.43–48.

R. Spence, 'Antipodean pavilion, house for an artist and his family in Mosman, Sydney' in *Architectural Review*, vol.191, 1149, November 1991, pp.46–50.

H. Beck, J. Cooper, 'Glenn Murcutt. Silver City Museum, Broken Hill' in *UME*, vol.1, fasc.1, 1992.

G. Murcutt, 'The Mining Museum of Broken Hill' in *Perspecta*, 27, 1992, pp.168–85.

H. Beck, J. Cooper, 'Broken Hill' in *Architectural Review*, vol.190, 1139, January 1992, pp.60–62.

F. Fromonot, 'Casa ristrutturata nel quartiere di Paddington' and 'Una casa nuova' in *Abitare*, vol.305, March 1992, pp.166–73.

P. Drew, 'Building sheltered pathways through the landscape: Glenn Murcutt and Australian Architecture quiet revolution' in *Mass*, vol.IX, spring 1992, pp.6–9.

F. Fromonot, 'Glenn Murcutt a Sydney; Ken Done, pittore' in *Abitare*, vol.310, September 1992, pp.158–67.

I. McDougall, 'Keeping the Faith'; F. Fromonot, 'Selected projects 1962–1992'; G. Murcutt, 'A vision for change' (text of his speech on receiving the RAIA Gold Medal 1992), in *Architecture Australia*, vol.81, 6, September–October 1992, pp.50–62.

'An oasis in the city – the Magney house' in *MD*, vol.38, 11, November 1992, pp.42–47.

J. Welsh, 'Sydney, Done residence. Outback fashion' in *Building Design*, 1104, 27, November 1992, pp.16, 17.

E.M. Farrelly, *Glenn Murcutt – Three houses*, Phaidon Press, London, 1993.

G. Jahn, *Contemporary Australian Architecture*, Craftsman House, Sydney, 1993.

S. Murray, 'A competitive grain of beauty' in *Transition*, 40, 1993, pp.76–85.

F. Fromonot, 'Glenn Murcutt, architecte solo en Australie' in *AMC*, February 1993, pp.26–29.

F. Fromonot, 'La raison du paysage' in *L'Architecture d'aujourd'hui*, 285, February 1993, special issue, pp.70–77.

P. Hyatt, 'Northern light' in *Steel Profile*, 46, December 1993, pp.2–11.

H. Rasch, 'Für Leben unterm Heissen Blechdach' in *Haüser*, no.3, 1994, pp.94–101.

H. Edquist, 'Mabo, Terra Nullius and the Architecture of Place' in *Monument*, vol.1, no.3, 1994, pp.71–74.

F. Fromonot, 'Glenn Murcutt's ecological eloquence' in *Progressive Architecture*, no.4, April 1994, pp.66–73.

F. Fromonot, 'Yirrkala, Australia: Banduk Marika' in *Abitare*, no.335, December 1994, pp.90–95.

F. Fromonot, 'Rationele architectuur in een oud landschap' in *Archis*, no.5, May 1995, pp.38–50.

H. Rasch, 'Geniestreich auf die Australische Art' in *Haüser*, no.1, 1995, pp. 42–49.

We would like to thank the following for their photographic services: Tom Balfour, Reiner Blunck, Penelope Clay, Powerhouse Museum, Max Dupain, Françoise Fromonot, Frank Gardner, Color Prints, Peter Hyatt, Geoff Lung, Trevor Mein, David Moore, Glenn Murcutt, Andrew Payne, Eric Sierins, Harry Sowden, Julius Shulman, Faye Walker and Kate Wimble.